ANALYZING VISUAL DATA

MICHAEL S. BALL
Staffordshire Polytechnic

GREGORY W. H. SMITH
University of Salford

Qualitative Research Methods
Volume 24

SAGE PUBLICATIONS
International Educational and Professional Publisher
Newbury Park   London   New Delhi

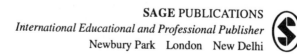

For information address:

SAGE Publications, Inc.
2455 Teller Road
Newbury Park, California 91320
E-mail: order@sagepub.com

SAGE Publications Ltd.
6 Bonhill Street
London EC2A 4PU
United Kingdom

SAGE Publications India Pvt. Ltd.
M-32 Market
Greater Kailash I
New Delhi 110 048 India

Printed in the United States of America

Library of Congress Cataloging-in-Publication Data

Ball, M. S. (Michael S.)
    Analyzing visual data/Michael S. Ball, Gregory W. H. Smith
        p. cm. — (Qualitative research methods; v. 24)
    Includes bibliographical references (p.   ).
    ISBN 0-8039-3434-3.   —ISBN 0-8039-3435-1 (pbk.)
    1. Social sciences—Research—Methodology. 2. Photography in the
social sciences—Interpretation. 3. Photographs—Psychological
aspects. I. Smith, Gregory W. H. II. Title. III. Series.
H62.B288   1992
001.4'225—dc20   92-7984
                                                    CIP

            00 01 02 03 10 9 8 7 6 5

Sage Production Editor: Judith L. Hunter

CONTENTS

EDITORS' INTRODUCTION

Ethnographic qualitative work routinely involves the systematic use of the senses and reflection on their varying role on the materials gathered and analyzed. However, it is rather clear that the sense of sight or observation is viewed as the primary sense in ethnographic work. This book carefully analyzes the role of vision and of visual data in qualitative work.

This work integrates the insights of anthropological, social psychological, and sociological approaches to the analysis of visual materials. Ball and Smith are careful to circumscribe their interests to the "secondary," or the perspective, theoretical viewpoint, or verbal accounts that are provided for the visual materials. They want to make the ". . .visual dimension used by filmmakers and members of society a topic of inquiry in its own right." They consider photographs as their primary illustrative materials, although they also discuss the content of visual representation, symbolic and structuralist analysis of visual materials, and the social organization of visual experience.

The theoretical purchase on materials they provide permits an exploration of the ways in which "experience" is converted in visual forms or representations and back. As the books by Manning and Gephart in this series have suggested, an underlying question to be addressed in qualitative work is not only how to describe social life, but also to undercover the organization of forms of experience.

—Peter K. Manning
John Van Maanen
Marc L. Miller

ACKNOWLEDGMENTS

The authors and publishers wish to acknowledge, with thanks, the following persons and organizations for permission to use the pictorial materials reproduced in this book:

The Association of Social Anthropologists of the Commonwealth; Helena Wayne (Malinowska); The Pitt Rivers Museum; The University of Chicago Press; Marilyn Strathern; Andrew Strathern; Bill Holm; Johsel Namkung; The Museum of the American Indian; Marion Boyars Publishers Ltd; Wesley W. Sharrock.

Mike Ball would like to thank the Department of Social Anthropology at the University of Manchester for an honorary visiting research fellowship that allowed the time for much of the early thinking about this book to develop. Both of us are grateful to John Van Maanen for his patient and helpful editorial work. We also wish to acknowledge the constant help, support, and encouragement given to us by David Jary, John Lee, Joel Richman, and Wes Sharrock. Responsibility for the text that follows, of course, remains entirely our own.

ANALYZING VISUAL DATA

MICHAEL S. BALL
Staffordshire Polytechnic
GREGORY W. H. SMITH
University of Salford

INTRODUCTION

This book can be located in the small but thriving academic subareas of visual anthropology and sociology. Its concerns are conveyed by the title. The social world is in part a seen world, available to most of its participants via the medium of vision. The appearance of the built environment, artifacts, persons, and courses of social action plays an indispensable role in the conduct of our daily lives, for these appearances have a variety of beliefs and expectations about the nature and workings of the world associated with them. For most people, some degree of competence at observation is a sine qua non of membership of society.

The visual mode has a significant role in the life of all human societies but the sheer diversity and commonplaceness of its forms in modern urban societies is noteworthy. As Gombrich (1960) suggests,

> Never before has there been an age like ours when the visual image was so cheap in every sense of the word. We are surrounded and assailed by posters

and advertisements, by comics and magazine illustrations. We see aspects of reality represented on the television screen and in the cinema, on postage stamps and on food packages. (p. 7)

Within the social sciences, the implications of the omnipresence of visual imagery and the ordinary viewing competence of human beings was first identified by Georg Simmel (1858-1918). In a celebrated passage in his *Soziologie* (1908/1921), Simmel claimed that of our five senses, "The eye has a uniquely sociological function" (p. 358). Simmel identifies some of the principal implications of humanity's occupancy of a seen world: how the mutual direct glance serves as a vehicle for conveying recognition, acknowledgment, understanding, intimacy, shame and so forth; how the intentions and moods of others may be visually read from facial expressions and bodily dispositions; how the role of "mere visual impression" (p. 360) increases in large-scale urban society. Simmel's insights have been developed in a range of ways, but his fundamental point about the enormous significance of the visual mode in social life is one we seek to pursue in this book.

Becker (1979) somewhat sardonically observed, "Visual social science isn't something brand new . . . but it might as well be" (p. 7). We contend that the seen world is amenable to anthropological and sociological investigation, and the purpose of this book is to outline how such investigations can be achieved. The book is animated by a concern with ways of doing the analysis of visual phenomena as distinct from the more standard illustrative inclusion of photographs in anthropological and sociological works. We promote the analysis of the seen world by suggesting how visual phenomena can serve as an investigative topic in contrast to their more common role as an illustrative resource (Zimmerman & Pollner, 1971). Visual phenomena can be investigated through a variety of theoretical frameworks, and an overall aim of the book is to explore the use and limitations of these frameworks. At the methodological level, we concentrate primarily upon qualitative methods, although quantitative methods are also considered. Publications in Sage's Qualitative Research Methods series have a distinct character, being succinct and cogent treatments of methodological matters, and the current volume is intended to conform to this character. This feature is reflected in our selection and inclusion of visual materials. For a book concerned with promoting the analysis of stored visual materials and the seen world, we somewhat surprisingly include only a limited collection of visuals, 16 photographs and 1 graph. The photographs included, however, are carefully selected, and the textual analysis is intended to grow out of close attention to the visual information encoded within them. Our photographs are thus not simply included for illustrative purposes, but intended to engage the reader in an analytical investigation of the visual.

Our book, then, is "theory-driven." It explores a range of theoretical frameworks for the analysis of visual phenomena: content analysis, symbolism, structuralism, cognitive anthropology, and ethnomethodology. Our reason for choosing to organize the book thus is that the theoretical framework sets an agenda for the types of researchable questions that can be addressed. All observation and investigation, lay and analytic, is theory-laden; there are no theory-free views of the world. The capacity of the approach to impose a set of theoretical relevancies and establish the frame for analysis is something we think must be constantly borne in mind. Hence, we place the theoretical horse before the analytical cart.

In the chapters that follow we show how the analysis of visual phenomena is structured by the theoretical framework adopted. Like any structure, there are enabling and constraining aspects to the frameworks used, and we consider their varying strengths and weaknesses. Theoretical frameworks exhibit certain of the characteristics of what Wittgenstein (1953) termed *language games,* in that the conceptual apparatus and vocabulary used shape the analysis. Each theoretical framework we consider suggests an investigative stance, and to a certain extent each is self-sufficient as a coherent and consistent analytical enterprise—a language game—that is locatable within an academic context or "form of life." The game metaphor has also been used in a similar manner by Anderson, Hughes, and Sharrock (1985), and it is one we find in certain respects preferable to the more usual emphasis on perspective.

We should make it clear that this book is principally intended to indicate what a range of theoretical orientations have to offer a qualitative methodological analysis of the seen world. The emphasis is on exploring what theoretical orientations offer, and how they have been used, alongside a treatment of their relationship to methods and data collection. The book is thus not exclusively concerned with presenting a "how-to" exposition of visual analysis, although to an extent it is intended to provide such guidance. "How-to" will be given a central place in a forthcoming work, but for now theoretical orientation has center stage because of its formative consequences for data collection and methods of investigation.

The Scope of the Book

The major form of visual representation addressed by our book is the still photograph. Although other visual representations such as sketches will not be neglected, it is photography that has been regarded by anthropologists and sociologists as the major way of representing the seen world. The powerful claim to realism presented by photography has made it an attractive tool for the anthropologist and sociologist: It appears to permit the rapid and faithful recording of visual phenomena. Photographs constitute still or frozen images of an instant. In order to explore the processual and sequential character of visible social arrangements—what Garfinkel (1968) has termed the "now you see it, now you don't" character of social life—the comparison of photographs and videotape is necessary, which we undertake in a forthcoming work.

A significant area of visual representation to which we devote only passing attention in this book is ethnographic film. This mode of representation consists of second-order constructs in that it is usually based on an already developed ethnographic account. The ethnographic film is typically a vehicle for the exposition of selected themes from the ethnographic account, which operates almost as the script for the film. It is noteworthy that the Royal Anthropological Institute's catalog of ethnographic films generally includes the name of the consultant anthropologist alongside that of the director. For example, anthropologist Thomas Gregor's (1977) work is referred to in the description of Carlos Pasini's *The Mehinacu*. Ethnographic films are usually founded on an ethnographic monograph that has typically been researched by conventional fieldwork techniques and informed by ethnographic theory.

We investigate visual representations and consider their uses in generating anthropological and sociological accounts. In this sense, our book addresses a fundamental set of issues to do with the ways a culture is visually available and the kinds of analysis that can be made of this visuality. Ethnographic film trades on the visual dimension as a resource for constructing its narrative; we want to make the visual dimension used by filmmakers *and* members of society a topic of inquiry in its own right. Our concerns, therefore, lie largely prior to the second-order matters addressed by ethnographic film makers.

Outline of Chapter Contents

CHAPTER 1: THE USE OF PHOTOGRAPHS IN A DISCIPLINE OF WORDS

This chapter highlights the visual availability of culture and considers how ethnographers have traditionally treated the seen world. It presents a brief historical review of the types and uses of visual materials (especially photographs) in anthropology and sociology, considering their status in research.

CHAPTER 2: ANALYZING THE CONTENT OF VISUAL REPRESENTATIONS

The application of content analysis to visual materials in anthropology and sociology is examined in chapter 2. Its uses and limitations are discussed and the prospects for a qualitative-oriented content analysis considered.

CHAPTER 3: SYMBOLIST AND STRUCTURALIST ANALYSES OF VISUAL REPRESENTATIONS

Chapter 3 reviews the application of the essentially qualitative methods of symbolism and structuralism, both separately and in combination.

CHAPTER 4: THE SOCIAL ORGANIZATION OF VISUAL EXPERIENCE

The concluding chapter examines how the ethnographic inquiries of cognitive anthropology and ethnomethodology investigates dimensions of the social organization of visual experience. Certain issues within anthropological post-modernism are explored, and some implications for an ethnographically based investigation of the seen world are indicated.

1. THE USE OF PHOTOGRAPHS IN A DISCIPLINE OF WORDS

Our primary concern in this book is to explore the use and potential of visual data—particularly photographs—for ethnographic investigation and analysis. Broadly conceived, ethnography is the study of culture: It seeks to provide a descriptive analysis of cultural arrangements and practices. In this book we pose the question, How can visual data be used to facilitate the ethnographic enterprise?

The Visual Dimension in Ethnography

Of the academic disciplines in which ethnographic investigation has flourished, anthropology has been more open to the employment of photography than sociology. Anthropology's traditional topic matter, non-Western cultures, are, after all, *visibly* different from the cultures in which many of its practitioners originate. Thus, it is not surprising that anthropologists were quick to appreciate the camera's virtues for their work. Ethnographically inclined sociologists have also perceived the camera's merits for their purposes, but in general terms, visual anthropology (see Collier & Collier, 1986) is a rather more developed specialism than visual sociology (see e.g., Becker, 1981).

Given the primarily descriptive concerns of ethnography, the precise record of material reality that photography provides is a powerful appeal. The camera operates by a mechanical process and there is therefore one important sense in which the camera cannot lie. Moreover, since the camera is a machine that is sensitive to the intentions of its operator, it permits selective and focused observation—unlike, for example, the audio tape recorder. Metaphorically speaking, the camera has a better "memory" than the human eye. Using photographs, the ethnographer has a relatively standard image to examine repeatedly. In contrast, the awareness of the ethnographer employing the conventional notebook and pencil recording technique can be "ground down" over time as familiarity with the culture grows (Collier & Collier, 1986).

Ethnographic reports are, however, usually presented in the written mode. Ordinary language and the more esoteric analytic vocabularies of anthropology and sociology constitute the terminology of published ethnography. In contrast, the conduct of ethnographic fieldwork may involve the experience of artifacts, beliefs, and practices by several of the ethnographer's senses. Indeed, vision is often primary, as the frequently overlooked metaphoric use of the term *observation* attests. These witnessings and observations are then transformed into a written account; experience is transformed into linguistic descriptions. The enormous symbolic power of language—it constitutes the basis of our rational faculty—is the obvious justification for this practice. The representation of culture thus takes place primarily through the medium of language. We do not wish to question this method of conducting ethnographic description and analysis, only to note its widespread acceptance as a convention and the consequent neglect of visual modes of representation that accompanies it. What we wish to problematicize is the issue, in Mead's (1975) phrasing of "using photographs in a discipline of words" an issue that in Tyler's (1986) equally felicitous locution, results in "language doing the work of eyes" (p. 137) in ethnographic work: The visual is mediated verbally, images are translated into words. This chapter surveys how photographs have been used in anthropology and sociology—disciplines of words—in order to examine the ways in which language has been allowed to do the work of eyes.

Early Uses of Photography in
Anthropology and Sociology

One anthropological use of photography in the nineteenth century was to document the physical characteristics of different social groups. Animated by Darwin's theory of evolution and the ethnological enterprise, anthropologists, often in collaboration with geologists, paleontologists, and archaeologists, endeavored to precisely describe the apparent physical features of the major racial groups (Mongol, Negro, Caucasian). In particular, photographs were used as an adjunct to the measurements made of body mass and skeletal size, which were believed to significantly vary among racial groups. These inquiries laid the foundation of what came to be known as anthropometry. An interest in the physical differences between racial groups persisted into early-twentieth-century anthropology before becoming the specialism of physical anthropology. Thus, for example, Radcliffe-Brown's study of the Andaman Islanders is described on the cover of a current paperback edition as "an investigation of the physical characteristics, language, culture and technology of a primitive society." In fact, only a small portion of the book is devoted to describing the physical features of the Andaman Islanders (Radcliffe-Brown, 1922, Plate V; see Figure 1.1).

Although visual sociology is a less developed specialism than visual anthropology, it too has a history dating back to the nineteenth century. Stasz (1979) discusses a brief but important episode in the history of U.S. sociology: the publication between 1896 and 1916 in the then-premier journal of the discipline, the *American Journal of Sociology,* of 31 articles employing photographs. These articles dealt with various aspects of U.S. life (playgrounds, schools, prisons, housing, work) from a predominantly social problems vantage. Stasz argues that most of these articles were written by socially concerned persons on the fringes of the discipline, and that the absence of photographic material in the journal after 1916 is evidence of its editors' intention to make it a forum for work concerned with the advancement of sociology as a science at the expense of wider social concerns. Many of these articles used photographs in a questionable way, but it remains the case today that major sociology journals in both Europe and the United States only rarely publish articles with photographs. The episode illustrates how the possibilities of photography for sociological analysis were at least broached in the early years of the discipline, although it has since remained a discipline

Figure 1.1. A man of the *Akar-Bale* tribe with South Andaman bow and arrows, wearing belt and necklace of netting and *Dentalium* shell. (Height 1,494 mm., 4 feet 9 inches). Photo from Radcliffe-Brown.

wedded to words. Sociologists seeking publication of papers employing pictorial materials usually have to turn to specialist journals such as the *International Journal of Visual Sociology.*

Standard Ethnographic Uses of Photography

Many significant anthropological ethnographies dating from the mid-1920s onward include photographs relating to the fieldwork. What is the purpose of their inclusion and the relationship, if any, between the photographs and the written text? It is difficult to generalize, but it seems to be the case that photographs are included in ethnographic reports more for evidential than analytical purposes. The photographs serve essentially presentational and illustrative purposes rather than providing a focus for a more sustained analysis of the visual dimensions of culture. Many of the photographs included in classic ethnographies suggest among other things that the ethnographer has been to the fieldwork setting and that the group and practices studied do indeed exist. Photographs of people and things stand as evidence in a way that pure narrative cannot. In many senses, visual information of what the people and their world looks like provides harder and more immediate evidence than the written word; photographs can authenticate a research report in a way that words alone cannot.

For an example of how this authentication operates, consider Malinowski's extensive use of photographs to illustrate among other things, ritual practices, everyday life, and material culture. In *The Sexual Life of Savages,* Malinowski (1929) includes an interestingly posed photograph of himself talking to a bewigged sorcerer, which provides in many senses harder evidence of his visit to the Trobriands than the stamp on his passport (Figure 1.2). A comparison of figures 1.1 and 1.2 is illuminating in so far as it visually reveals a distinct change in anthropological methodology and orientation, from presenting people as anthropometrical exhibits, to showing the ethnographer in-there-with-them, as is characteristic of ethnographic anthropology.

Many of the classical anthropological ethnographies use photographs to economically show the visual differences of alien culture. For instance, consider the extensive use of photographs by Evans-Pritchard (1937, 1940), Bateson (1936), Firth (1936), Gluckman (1965), and Turner (1967). In U.S. cultural anthropology, where general ethnological concerns held sway, as indicated by the links between the discipline and ethnologically oriented museums, photographs and moving film were regarded as important and

Figure 1.2. Ethnographer with a man in a wig. Photo from Malinowski.

legitimate records of artifacts and human conduct. Boas and his associates, including Hunt (see, for example, Boas & Hunt, 1905, 1908) and, indirectly, Curtis (1915), developed an extensive collection of the material and nonmaterial culture of the Northwest Coast American Indians that has provided a valuable resource for subsequent generations of anthropologists (e.g., Lévi-Strauss, 1983).

Ethnological multidisciplinary impulses are still alive in modern anthropological studies like Chagnon's (1974) investigation of the Yanomamo. Chagnon made many hours of moving film and took large numbers of photographs. In addition to the pictures of Yanomamo everyday activities, he presents a series of 156 identity photographs of the residents of

Mishimishimabowei-teri in 1971, a form of visual census (see Chagnon, 1974, Appendix E), which he suggests he will use in subsequent visits to establish mortality.

We have argued that as part of ethnographic reports, photographs are largely ancillary to the principal analytical purposes of the work. They are usually presented as a descriptive resource rather than a visual topic of inquiry. There is, however, also a class of anthropological works in which the phenomenon investigated is itself clearly a visual one that benefits from visual representation: the cross-cultural study of the visual arts, plastic and graphic, costume, self-decoration, masks, architecture, religious iconography, and other aspects of material culture.

A classical example is Haddon's (1895) investigation of the origin, evolution, and decay of art forms. Haddon's book clearly benefits from the inclusion of a number of sketches of artifacts and designs. Similarly Boas's (1927) book *Primitive Art* also benefits from a visual representation of the phenomena. The visuals included by Boas are a mixture of sketches (more than 300) and photographs (15). Even a casual reading of the book suggests that the inclusion of visual materials is closely tied to the textual descriptions, and the visual materials serve the purpose of enhancing the reader's understanding of the styles in question. The same is true of more recent anthropological studies of art, which make extensive use of photographs (e.g., Cordwell, 1979), and publications of the Institute of Religious Iconography.

Prestigious anthropology journals such as *Man* are rather more willing to include photographs than their sociology counterparts, but it is still true that visually oriented articles are not frequently published. Instead, as in sociology, such papers are hived off to specialist journals such as *Studies in Visual Communication.*

We have suggested a twofold distinction within the standard uses of photography in anthropology: (1) as part of ethnographic reports, and (2) as a resource for the examination of visual phenomena. In comparison, the use of photographs is even less common in sociology. Only a very small proportion of sociological papers and monographs have photographic materials integrated in their published format. The exception that confirms the rule are those introductory texts, largely designed for U.S. undergraduate audiences, that incorporate varying amounts of "topical" photographs (see Coser, Nock, Steffan, & Rhea, 1987, for an excellent example). The rule appears to be that sociology is primarily a verbally rather than visually communicated discipline; or, to be more precise, that tables, graphs, and histograms appear to be the sociologist's preferred visual data. Photographs are occasionally found on the covers of sociology books, but few substantial research studies in sociology have used photographs at all, let alone as a source of data for sociological analysis.

This situation holds even if attention is restricted to the ethnographic sociologies. Despite the early example of the *American Journal of Sociology* papers published around the turn of the century, few of the classics of the Chicago School contain photographic data. Anderson's (1923) monograph contains a dozen or so photographs of street scenes and figures typical of hobo life in the 1920s, but the captions are bare ("A dining room on the 'main stem,' " "Employment bureaus") and the pictures are not, in the main, directly referred to in the text. Here, as is so often the case in both anthropology and sociology, pictures serve a simply decorative and illustrative function: They *show* aspects of hobo life, without analyzing in detail what the picture depicts. . A somewhat more sophisticated use of photographic illustrations is found in Thrasher's (1927) *The Gang*. Thrasher's book contains nearly 40 photographs, many depicting the groups of boys who formed the gangs that were the object of his investigation. But in addition to a title for each photograph, Thrasher provides background information and analysis of the persons and events depicted, a commentary that often runs to several sentences. References to specific chapters of his book and to numbered documentary sources cited in the text are also included. With the explicitly reformist tone of the commentaries, the photographs in Thrasher's work stand squarely in that tradition of U.S. documentary photography beginning with Jacob Riis in the 1890s and running through to the work of Walker Evans and Dorothea Lange in the 1930s (Riis, 1890; Agee & Evans, 1941; Ohrn, 1980).

Sociology's endeavor to establish itself as a distinct academic discipline, however, meant that from the 1920s it concentrated upon its own theories and methods and relinquished links with neighboring intellectual traditions, such as documentary photography. As a result, photographs became even rarer in sociological ethnographies: The success of studies like *Street Corner Society* (Whyte, 1943) and *Asylums* (Goffman, 1961) was accomplished, at the textual level, by verbal rather than pictorial means.

Exemplary Uses of Photographs as Data

Our major complaint about the few sociological works and the rather more numerous anthropological studies that do use photographic material is that the materials are underanalyzed, generally serving as little more than illustrative devices. This tendency we have described as the standard use of photography, and it is most clearly seen in those ethnographies in which an extensive written report is accompanied by a dozen or so photographs apparently intended only to vivify the serious work of ethnographic analysis accomplished by the written text. This practice is the basis of Ruby's (1976) observation that taking photographs is only occasionally a way of *doing* anthropology, for anthropologists have not commonly entertained the possibility of doing serious analysis of their photographs.

The major exception to the general trend remains Bateson and Mead's (1942) classic, *Balinese Character: A Photographic Analysis.* The book contains 759 photographs arranged into 100 "plates," each of which depicts an element of Balinese culture. The book was the product of 2 years' fieldwork carried out in 1936-1939 on the island of Bali, in which time Bateson and Mead amassed 25,000 still photographs and 22,000 feet of movie film. They worked as a team, with Bateson filming and Mead interviewing and taking notes.

Balinese Character is an example of the then-popular area of research into the relation of culture to personality. Bateson and Mead's primary concern was to describe the ethos of the Balinese. By *ethos* they refer to the ways in which the instincts and emotions of individuals are shaped by culture—"a culturally standardized system of organization of the instincts and emotions of individuals" (p. xi). Because the ethos of a culture is not easy to communicate, Bateson and Mead elected to articulate its elements in pictures as well as words, hoping each would add to the other.

Aspects of primary socialization among the Balinese constitute a significant part of Bateson and Mead's study. One common pattern of childrearing involves a mother stimulating the interest of her small child, pulling his penis or offering him her nipple to feed on. As the child's interest develops she may intentionally divert her attention elsewhere, giving the child to believe that she is no longer interested in his activity. As the child grows older, the mother's teasing becomes more complex: She will rebuff her child's anger and jealousy, refuse to take it seriously, perhaps cosset or even breast-feed someone else's child in her own child's presence. To Westerners, Balinese parents make inadequate responses to the climaxes of the child's love and anger: Instead of meeting the child's emotions head on, they sidestep them. The consequence of such childrearing is that the child learns to withdraw from situations, becomes reticent about being drawn into activity, and may even appear to lack social responsiveness. The serene, cool, level-headed, equanimous character of the Balinese owes its origins to these childrearing practices. Bateson and Mead are able to tell *and* show exactly what these practices consist in and thereby present richer ("thicker") ethnographic descriptions than would be possible by words alone (see Bateson & Mead, 1942, plates 39, 47, and 69).

To reiterate: Our complaint about ethnographic reports centers on their neglect of photographic material as a serious source of data worthy of analysis. In a sense, this argument is a variant of the ethnomethodological distinction between topic and resource. Photographs usually only serve illustrative functions for anthropological work or at best stand as constituents of slide-show travelogues. What makes Bateson and Mead's work exemplary and ground breaking is its use of photographs as topics of investigation, and indeed why it still repays close study is its authors' sensitivity to "the steps by which workers in a new science solve piecemeal their problems of description and analysis" (Bateson & Mead, 1942, p. xii).

Bateson and Mead show how photographic material, judiciously accompanied by a commentating text, can deepen ethnographic understanding. Another study that well exemplifies the use of photographs as data is Goffman's (1979) *Gender Advertisements*. Goffman presents more than 500 photographs, drawn mainly from illustrated newspaper and magazine advertisements. The aim is to analyze "gender displays": the culturally conventional expressions of sex-class membership that are ordinarily available to us "at a glance." He decisively rejects the doctrine that gender displays reflect hidden or underlying biological or social structural characteristics. Instead he contends that there is "only a schedule for the portrayal of gender . . . only evidence of the practice between the sexes of choreographing behaviorally a portrait of relationship" (p. 8). Commonsensically, gender displays simply honor the presumed immutable differences between the sexes; for Goffman, they constitute those differences.

The analysis of gender as a phenomenon that is manifested in the details of interactional conduct and recognizable to members of society as such is facilitated by a ceremonial model. In the first of the book's three sections, Goffman argues that the rituals of gender display serve to affirm basic social arrangements (keeping women in their place) and to present ultimate conceptions of humanity and the world (our "essential" gender identity). His central thesis is that gender relationships are permeated by a behavioral vocabulary typical of parent-child relationships. The "orientation license," "protective intercession," "benign control," and "non-person treatment" that parents extend to children also characterize the socially situated treatment of women by men. Thus, "ritually speaking, females are equivalent to subordinate males and both are equivalent to children" (Goffman, 1979, p. 5).

Goffman then examines the varying senses in which pictures can and cannot be regarded as depictions of some "real" state of affairs. Goffman is well aware that advertisements present a distorted view of the world, one that is prettier and more affluent than everyday reality. Yet because advertisements trade on the same viewing competence that we all unthinkingly exercise in daily life, and because they are deliberately contrived to permit unobstructed and unambiguous viewing, they provide a rich fund of data for the student of gender display. In Goffman's view, the advertiser's hype is to "hyper-ritualize" everyday gender displays.

Goffman's third and longest section is devoted to a pictorial analysis of the presentation of gender in advertisements. Using pictorial materials has the considerable advantage of allowing subtle features of gender displays to be exhibited where words alone would stand deficient. Although this is true of other works that have used this strategy, such as *Balinese Character,* the innovation marked by *Gender Advertisements* lies in its utilization of naturally occurring or indigenous photographs rather than those taken by the researcher. Indeed, a central rationale for this study is that the pictures are part of the society they describe.

In the pictorial section of *Gender Advertisements* Goffman exploits the reader's ordinary viewing competence with what he terms the "glimpsed world" in order to promote the analysis of gender displays. Analytic points are made through relatively brief written interpretations and extensive arrays of pictures. The reader has to read Goffman's analysis and then inspect the collection of pictures that give it substance. The reader's own ordinary viewing competence is drawn upon to give specific sense to Goffman's analytic interpretations. Characteristically, Goffman is anything but heavy-handed in presenting these interpretations. For example, in noting the difference between how fathers and sons, and mothers and daughters, are represented in advertising pictures, Goffman suggests "Boys, as it were, have to push their way to manhood and problematic effort is involved" (1979, pp. 38-39, followed by pictures 89-92), whereas, "Girls merely have to unfold" (pictures 93-99). The mutual elaboration of written and pictorial elements of the text that the reader must undertake to make sense of it all is *provoked* by the laconicity of the written commentary.

Photography and Realism

If a case is to be made that visual data can play a useful role in ethnographic analysis, then the issue of realism must be directly addressed. As will be evident from the next chapter, on content analysis, "objectivity" is the major criterion of the adequacy of positivistic researches. In contrast "realism"—a commitment to "tell it like it is," to record the reality of what has taken place—is the major criterion of the adequacy of ethnographic investigations (Bittner, 1973). So, in what senses can photography offer the ethnographer realistic representations for investigation? This is the notoriously thorny problem of realism. We shall return to this issue throughout the book, but because of its centrality for ethnographic work, some preliminary considerations are required. We examine these under four headings: (1) the distinctive features of photographs relative to other forms of visual representation; (2) the staging and faking of photographs; (3) aesthetics, realism, and documentary; and (4) contexts, captions, and viewers.

1. THE DISTINCTIVE FEATURES OF THE PHOTOGRAPH

How do photographs differ from other forms of visual representation, such as paintings, drawings, and sketches? These forms are acknowledged to be stylized visual representations and not mere "copies" of whatever they portray. They mediate the visual features of the world through the consciousness of the artist who constructs them. As John Berger (1989) perceptively suggested, "Photographs do not translate from appearances. They quote them" (p. 96).

Photographs are made in an instant and represent that instant. They possess a credibility that artistic representations lack, arising from the mechanical and chemical basis of the photographic process; the camera as a "mirror with a memory." Photographs are thus linked to the world's appearances by a "binding" or necessary tie, and it is this feature that lends credence to whatever they depict as somehow "actual" and to the belief that they mirror "reality." The mirror is a powerful visual metaphor for exploring realism, as evidenced by Rorty's (1979) influential *Philosophy and the Mirror of Nature*. Science has been concerned to hold up a cultural mirror to nature. But mirrors, even metaphorical ones, can also distort, as debates around postmodernism indicate. We will return to the metaphor of the mirror in the current and subsequent chapters. But even the mirror-like character of photographs will not guarantee their realism, for as Tagg (1988) reminds us, "Ask yourself, under what conditions would a photograph of the Loch Ness Monster or an Unidentified Flying Object become acceptable as proof of their existence?" (p. 160). Clearly, other issues are involved, which we consider next.

2. THE STAGING AND FAKING OF PHOTOGRAPHS

Bittner (1973) suggested that the ethnographer is "a visitor whose main interest in things is to *see* them, and to whom, accordingly, all things are primarily *exhibits*" (p. 121). But what if the photographed exhibit is interfered with in some way, either by the action of the photographer to stage or fake the picture, or by those who use the photograph for their own ends? As Berger (1989) suggested, to make a photograph "lie" in this way involves processes extraneous to photography (touching up, collage, and other ways of tampering with the image). Stalin's alleged removal of Trotsky from a historically significant photograph of Lenin as orator is one celebrated example of these practices at work; one that adds a curiously ironic twist to the adage that the camera never lies. Thus, if a picture is to be regarded as "true," then the circumstances of its production and the conclusions we wish to draw from it must be taken into account (cf. Becker, 1978, p. 12). In the photographs included in anthropological texts, persons may be "posed," artifacts "arranged," and activities "staged." Often, however, we are not provided with information about the circumstances of the photograph's production; ethnographically informed viewers need to be aware of this further facet of photographic credibility.

3. AESTHETICS, REALISM, AND DOCUMENTARY

Realism is also a major concern of documentary photography, a genre that is almost coterminous with the history of photography itself. As one distinguished exponent, Dorothea Lange, put it: "Documentary photography records the social scene of our time. It mirrors the present and documents for the future" (quoted in Ohrn, 1980, p. 37).

Documentary photography seeks to mirror and report a particular state of affairs. The documentary photograph visually displays the "facts" of some situation. The photograph can be designed to encourage us as viewers to come to some conclusion about how the world is and the way it works; these visual "facts" can, for instance, concern the experience of disadvantaged and oppressed individuals and groups in society, portrayed in a way aimed at enabling the viewer to empathize with the situation of the subjects (Becker, 1975). Unlike much social scientific work that employs photography, documentary explicitly fuses descriptive and persuasive concerns. The fusion is achieved through the aesthetics of documentary. Although documentary is wedded to the notion of photography as reportage, even its most enthusiastic proponents recognize its aesthetic dimension: Choices have to be made about pose, light, composition, lenses, filters, types of film, shutter speeds, and so forth. Indeed, it is sometimes argued that attention to these matters can serve to heighten the realism of the photograph, to enhance the clarity of its message.

Thus documentary's claim to realism needs to be approached cautiously: It is a professional ideology. In its most naive form, documentary realism rests upon two assumptions that are open to challenge: (1) that cameras take pictures and the camera never lies, and (2) that the world is as it appears to be and the camera faithfully records and mirrors those appearances. Against the first assumption it must be remembered that it is people and not cameras who take pictures (Ruby, 1976, p. 6). Sontag (1979) summarized current theory about this aspect of photographic practice: "To take a good photograph, runs the common claim, one must already see it. That is, the image must exist in the photographer's mind, at or before the moment when the negative was exposed" (p. 117). Against the second assumption it must be emphasized that photographs are not unambiguous records of reality: The sense viewers make of them depends upon cultural assumptions, personal knowledge, and the context in which the picture is presented.

4. CONTEXTS, CAPTIONS, AND VIEWERS

Photographic literacy is learned: Photographs are made sense of by a viewing subject and thus do not straightforwardly reflect reality. Bushmen studied by Herskovits required instruction before they could make any sense of photographs he showed them of themselves (Sekula, 1975, p. 85; see also Barley, 1986, p. 97). Photographs are neither "raw" data nor "brute" facts, but unavoidably require interpretive work on the part of the viewer. But there is also the danger that in viewing photographs "ethnocentric judgements" (Ruby, 1976, p. 7) may emerge from the viewer's own cultural knowledge. What is found in the picture is conditioned by the cultural knowledge the viewer brings to the viewing. Since photographs, like any other text, are polysemic, any interpretation the viewer makes will not "exhaust" the significance that might be attributed to the photograph. Moreover, as with any other type of text (cf. Morley, 1980, 1981), the sense that is made of a photograph will be structured by the viewer's social affiliations.

These issues can be illustrated by reference to a photograph of cattle byre construction included in Evans-Pritchard's (1940) classic ethnography of the Nuer (Figure 1.3). The caption provided under the photograph ("building a cattle byre") is a clue that directs us to view the photograph in a certain way,

Figure 1.3. Building a cattle byre (Eastern Jikany). Photo from Evans-Pritchard.

and coupled with the visual information that people are still engaged in working on the byre, suggests that the building is not completed. From this we are able to guess how it might be completed, what it might look like and the rest. This ability is, however, based upon our general cultural understandings and not theirs, our knowledge of such matters as building, construction, thatching, and the like, and not on a detailed understanding of Nuer equivalents. It is only possible to make even this much sense of Nuer byre construction by applying our own cultural knowledge to the visual materials and engaging in what Garfinkel (1967) would term practical reasoning, but practical reasoning derived from our culture and not theirs.

Three further distinctions might help us to appreciate the issues at stake in photographic realism. We can differentiate between (1) what is given in the photograph—its *content*; (2) whatever the photograph is of—its *referent*; and (3) the presentation of the photograph once made—the *context* in which it appears and the use made of it. We have already considered some of the problematic aspects of the relation between the photograph and its referent. As the Nuer illustration shows, the context in which a photograph appears is of significance in determining the sense we make of it. Family snapshots are regarded in a different light from photographs appearing in art galleries or those found in daily newspapers: The physical and social context in which the photograph is placed is of consequence when we seek to make sense of the photographic image. Signorile (1987) drew attention to the significant sense-making work done by captions. The relation of written text to photograph in ethnographic work is an area worthy of close scrutiny: As we have endeavored to show above, few ethnographies attain the complementary balance between text and photograph accomplished by Goffman (1979) in *Gender Advertisements* where the arrays of photographs depict details of gender display that would be difficult to put into words.

In diverse ways, these aspects of realism inform the subsequent chapters, in which we examine some of the major modes of analyzing visual data in anthropology and sociology. Our next chapter considers the leading social science method for textual analysis, content analysis.

2. ANALYZING THE CONTENT OF VISUAL REPRESENTATIONS

The visual material of interest to us in this book, primarily photographs, but to a lesser extent drawings and paintings, constitute part of a larger class of data known as documentary sources. These data include various forms of written reports and documents, audio recordings of speech and music, and visual records in the form of photographs, films, sketches, and the like, which can be put to a wide range of uses in social scientific research (see e.g., Mann, 1985, pp. 66-95; Platt, 1981; Scott, 1990). The major *systematic* and *empirical* method that has been developed for analyzing documentary data is content analysis. The modern version of the method emerged in the early twentieth century and was codified into its canonical form by Berelson (1952) in his *Content Analysis in Communication Research*.

For Berelson, content analysis is "a research technique for the objective, systematic and quantitative description of the manifest content of communication" (p. 18). Studies employing content analysis have overwhelmingly concentrated on written rather than audio or visual records, using, for example, organizational files (Wheeler, 1969), newspapers (Williams, 1976), periodical and ephemeral literature, and the like. Communication is considered to consist of a flow of messages from a transmitter to a receiver; thus, from an author to a readership, from a television program to its audience, or from a photograph to its viewer. It is the "manifest"—that is, the obvious, palpable, self-evident—features of the message that are of relevance to content analysis, not its latent or hidden dimensions. Thus content analysis is primarily limited to what is expressly communicated by some document rather than the motives animating the construction of the document or the responses that persons make to it (Berelson, 1952, p. 16; see also Holsti, 1969, pp. 12-14).

The method claims to offer an "objective," "systematic," and "quantitative" (Berelson, 1952, pp. 16-17) analysis of documentary content. The objectivity of content analysis resides in the devising of precisely and clearly defined categories to apply to the material analyzed in accordance with explicitly formulated rules of procedure. In principle, different analysts using the same categories and rules would obtain identical results from their analysis of any given body of data; therein lies the reliability of the method. The rules of procedure serve to minimize the influence of the individual analyst's disposition and preconceptions. The requirement that content analysis is systematic means that *all* the material relevant to the investigation must be analyzed, not just a selection designed to support a preferred hypothesis. Content analysis is also primarily a quantitative technique in that it aims to establish the frequency with which certain categories or themes appear in the material investigated. This quantitative dimension is facilitated by assigning numerical values to category or theme frequencies and is a basic characteristic of the method; there is also a variant of content analysis with a qualitative orientation, which we consider later.

Content Analysis of Visual Representation:
Two Studies of Fashion

How can the principles of content analysis be applied to visual materials? In this section, we have selected two studies of fashion to illustrate the application of content analysis to visual materials: Richardson and Kroeber's (1940) paper on changes in women's dress and Robinson's (1976) paper on shifts in the shaving and trimming of men's beards. Use of the method involves six basic steps: (1) selecting a topic and determining a research problem; (2) selecting a documentary source; (3) devising a set of analytic categories; (4) formulating an explicit set of instructions for using the categories to code the material; (5) establishing a principled basis for sampling the documents; and (6) counting the frequency of a given category or theme in the documents sampled.

1. SELECTING A TOPIC AND DETERMINING A RESEARCH PROBLEM

The first step in any scientific inquiry is the selection of a topic for investigation and the determination of a "research problem." Both studies consider aspects of the role of fashion in social life, a topic that has long interested sociologists (e.g., Simmel, 1957; Sapir, 1931; Konig, 1973). Richardson and Kroeber examined women's evening or formal dress in Western Europe and the United States, and Robinson investigated men's facial hair. They attempted to provide precise knowledge of the fluctuations in adornment that lie at the heart of fashion:

> This study is an attempt to define stylistic changes in an objective and quantitative manner. (Richardson & Kroeber, 1940, p. 11)

> This report represents the result of a careful sampling of the comparative frequencies over time of men's choices of forms of grooming of their facial hair. (Robinson, 1976, p. 1133)

The research problem for both studies was essentially descriptive: Are there patterns in the fashioning of women's dress and men's facial hair that can be discerned and measured? Content analysis purports to offer a method for providing a quantitative and objective description of these patterns.

2. SELECTING A DOCUMENTARY SOURCE

The next step in content analysis involves the identification of a documentary source (or sources) as an appropriate research site (i.e., relevant to the research problem). Here we consider fashion, a highly visual social phenomenon in which an element of display is always prominent.

Richardson and Kroeber used a variety of sources of data. Although the study covers the 332 years from 1605 to 1936, the soundest part of their empirical work is for the period 1787-1936, based on dated fashion plates in first lithographic and then photographic form. For the period prior to 1787, some rather less satisfactory data sources, engravings and portrait paintings, were drawn upon. Plainly, there are technological and historical restrictions on the data that are available and that can be selected for analysis. Robinson's study is explicitly modeled after Richardson and Kroeber, but differs from their work in relying on a single data source, the *Illustrated London News*. This magazine, published continuously throughout the sample period 1842-1972, presented the investigator with a rich source of pictures of men's faces.

3. DEVISING A SET OF CATEGORIES

The categories into which the content is to be coded are plainly central parts of the analytical process. As Berelson (1952) observed, "Content analysis stands or falls by its categories . . . since the categories contain the substance of the investigation, a content analysis can be no better than its system of categories" (p. 147). There are certain general criteria to be satisfied by all categories for a sound content analysis to be produced (cf. Holsti, 1969, pp. 95-100). First of all, the categories must reflect and be sensitive to the research problem. Richardson and Kroeber's research problem, the quantitative description of changes in women's dress fashions, is expressed in six measures: (1) length of dress, (2) length of waist, (3) depth of décolletage, (4) width of skirt, (5) width of waist, and (6) width of décolletage. Robinson's investigation of frequencies of types of facial hair grooming uses a schedule of five categories: (1) sideburns alone, (2) sideburns and mustache in combination, (3) beard, (4) mustache alone, and (5) clean-shaven. In each case, the categories chosen appropriately reflect the research problem.

Further requirements are that categories are mutually exclusive and exhaustive of the content under consideration. It is important that any element of the content is coded under one and only one category and that the category system is sufficiently comprehensive to provide space for every relevant aspect of content. Both studies meet these requirements.

4. FORMULATING AN EXPLICIT SET OF CODING RULES

Any given instance of content has to be coded, that is, allocated to one (and only one) category. Sometimes, however, a given item of content may be ambiguous and fall between two or more categories, and for that reason, it is essential that categories are sufficiently explicit to provide coders with clear instructions about how to deal with the problematic item. Sometimes decision rules have to be formulated to handle such ambiguities. Thus in

Richardson and Kroeber (1940), we find that "length of waist" is measured by the "Distance from the mouth to the minimum diameter across the waist. The girdle, or the lower edge of the corsage part of the dress, may coincide with this or lie above or below this diameter" (p. 112). More prosaically, Robinson (1976) deemed it necessary to define a beard as "any amount of whiskers centering on the chin" (p. 1134).

5. SAMPLING THE DOCUMENTS

Some selection of the material to be analyzed is usually necessary in order to ensure that a properly representative sample is obtained. Richardson and Kroeber (1940) attempted to acquire at least 10 pictures for each year; they admit encountering difficulty in reaching this number for the years prior to 1844, however (p. 133). Robinson aimed for a much larger annual total—100—and indeed in one year managed to obtain a total of 1,730 observations. Both studies excluded certain data from analysis: Richardson and Kroeber used only full-face or almost full-face figures because figures in profile could not provide all the required measurements (p. 112). Robinson excluded group photographs, advertisements, royalty, and non-Europeans, as each of these categories presented sources of bias to his sample of mainly British gentlemen "prominent in one way or another in their nation's affairs" (1976, p. 1134). The dating of Robinson's material was unproblematic because it all derived from a periodical publication. This was not true of Richardson and Kroeber's material, and they made knowledge of the date of each picture they analyzed "an absolute requirement" (1940, p. 112). In these ways, the researchers attempted to guard against the entry of atypical data into their research design.

6. COUNTING THE FREQUENCIES OF THE CATEGORIES

A count must be made of how often the categories appear in the content under investigation. The information thus obtained can be readily presented in tables or graphs, the practice adopted in the studies we reviewed: Richardson and Kroeber, for example, present 11 graphs and 29 tables to document shifts in the dimensions of women's dress. It is noteworthy that tables and graphs are the only visual data to figure in both research reports. The provision of examples of the data is deemed superfluous to the aims of content analysis; what is relevant is the tabular and graphical representation of the findings of the research. Moreover, much of the material collected in large-scale content analysis readily lends itself to cross-tabulation and significance testing, and here the researcher has been powerfully aided by the computer (see Gerbner, Holsti, Krippendorff, Paisley, & Stone, 1969; Krippendorff, 1980).

The principal finding of both studies reviewed here was to discover evidence for wavelike fluctuations in Western female dress and European male tonsorial styles. Richardson and Kroeber (1940) concluded that there is an alternating cycle of approximately 50 years duration between the minima and maxima of the basic dimensions of women's dress. Thus, the periodicity of the wave is about 100 years (p. 148). In addition, they found evidence to distinguish between periods of high and low variability of style. Robinson's study also furnished evidence of a century-long fashion wave-length, in this case computed from the average of the sideburns and mustaches, beards, and mustaches. Robinson reported a remarkable correspondence between the Richardson-Kroeber skirt-width wave and his own beard wave (see Figure 2.1).

How can these wavelike patterns best be explained? Richardson and Kroeber did not address this question in an extended way, preferring to stay close to descriptive concerns. The causes of the century-long wave periodicity of fashions are not given, and the authors caution us that data gathered for other civilizations may reveal very different patterns. The authors are confident, however, that they have detected evidence of a supraindividual, cultural patterning of changes in fashion, a patterning that cannot be accounted for by stock social psychological explanations of imitation, emulation, and competition. Robinson (1976) goes a step further and tries to explain why the wave has a duration of a century (pp. 1138-1139). Fashions of the preceding generations are often considered ugly or distasteful by the current generation. As long as there are numbers of people who follow a superseded fashion, that fashion will be looked on askance by the current generation. The distasteful associations of the superseded fashion will take approximately a century to disappear, or roughly a lifetime plus a generation.

An Appraisal of the Utility
of Content Analysis

For studies such as those reviewed above, content analysis has several virtues. First of all, it is a standardized technique that permits the processing of large amounts of data covering long time spans. Moreover, it is an unobtrusive research method, avoiding the problems of researcher effects

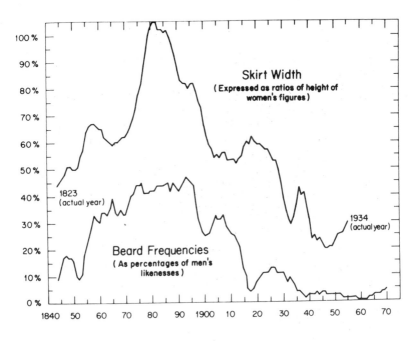

Figure 2.1. Skirt width and beard frequency fluctuations (Robinson, 1976, p. 1137).

on the data that are inherent in reactive research methods such as interviewing. It suffers from certain shortcomings, however, the most serious of which involve the issues of manifest and latent content, data fragmentation, and quantification. For ethnographically inclined researchers, these issues set limits on the usefulness of the method for the analysis of visual representations.

MANIFEST AND LATENT CONTENT

Berelson (1952) sought to restrict content analysis to what is manifestly apparent in the communicative message, excluding implicit or latent meanings from the coding operation. Our two studies stayed close to this constraint, but accompanying losses should not be ignored.

To meet the constraint, a clearly defined category system must plainly state the characteristics of content that are to qualify as instances of a given category (cf. Robinson's definition of a beard, above). As we have seen, every effort is made to treat coding as a mechanical procedure in which content is matched to category so that the coder need only inspect the manifest content of the data (e.g., a photograph) for the relevant features specified by the category system (clean-shavenness, beard, etc). It is important that the coder make no attempt to interpret the data in any wider way, such as by trying to recover the communicator's intent in publishing *this* picture showing a man *thusly* composed, because that would result in the coder speculating about latent meanings. But for some analysts of communication (e.g., Glassner & Corzine, 1982), the insistence upon coding only manifest content is too restrictive. These analysts argued that excessive emphasis on standardized technique can result in reliability being bought at the expense of validity. The significance of the communicative message may lie less in its manifest content than in the context in which it occurs.

DATA FRAGMENTATION

The characteristics articulated by the category system may or may not correspond to the categories that members of the society employ to understand the communicative message. Moreover, categorization isolates those elements of the communicative message determined by the analyst's theoretical relevancies (e.g., "length of waist," "width of waist"), whereas members of a society interpret a picture as a complete gestalt, representing, for example, "a fashionable young woman." Content analysis, by virtue of the methodological constraint of focusing upon manifest content, tends to break up instances of the communicative message into their elements, and it is solely the presence, absence, or frequency of these elements that is deemed relevant to the investigation. Content analysis is thus a research technique that in serving the theoretical purposes of the analyst (e.g., attempting to uncover historical patterns in fashion), isolates and atomizes its data, fragmenting the content of communication and effectively decontextualizing the message—a process that phenomenologists refer to as losing the phenomenon, or failing to respect the originary right of all data (cf. Waksler, 1986).

It follows that content analysis cannot properly appreciate the symbolic character of communication as it is naturally experienced, despite claims to the contrary by some content analysts (e.g., Krippendorff [1980], who maintains—without adequate demonstration—that it is quite possible for content analysis to be conducted in a manner "homorphic to the symbolic process in reality" [p. 31]). Moreover, communication content is only ever dealt with in the elemental units of the category system, not as a totality or natural whole. Content analysis behavioralizes its data in the interest of testing a scientifically formulated hypothesis. Readers of the *Illustrated London News* do not see a photograph as portraying a man with a mustache, however, but rather, for example, a portrait of Mr. X, an up-and-coming politician. An appreciation of communication content in its totality is one hallmark of symbolism and structuralism, the analytical schemes considered in the next chapter; a sensitivity to the social context in which the communicative message occurs is a feature of ethnomethodological work examined in the chapter that follows. These approaches show that it is possible to go beyond the manifest aspects of communication content, and to do so in a disciplined and systematic way.

QUANTIFICATION AND QUALITATIVE CONTENT ANALYSIS

Berelson (1952) argued that content analysis is an *essentially* quantitative research technique, and the two studies we have reviewed are representative in this respect. Content of communication is construed in quantitative terms, and what is taken as significant in the coded content is what occurs most frequently. For critics of various theoretical persuasions (e.g., Cicourel, 1964; Burgelin, 1972; Sumner, 1979), a major problem with content analysis is that repetition becomes the mark of significance. What is important, what is noteworthy in communication content is, for example, that 47% of the men who appeared in the *London Illustrated News* in the 5 years centering on 1892 wore beards. But repetition or frequency is a poor guide to the communicative significance or meaning of a particular item. What does wearing a beard indicate about a man around 1892 in England? Does it suggest respectability or wisdom or roguishness? A content analysis cannot address this kind of question.

Moreover, there are circumstances where frequency of a measure of significance can be positively misleading. In a popular film, to take an example from Burgelin (1972), a gangster may commit dozens of evil deeds, all of which may be "redeemed" in the audience's eyes by a single, splendidly heroic act in the final scene (p. 319). A count of antisocial and prosocial acts would not begin to get close to the meaning of the gangster's conduct in the film. Rather than viewing significance in frequency terms, structuralism argues "that the meaning of what is frequent is only revealed by opposition to what is rare" (Burgelin, 1972, p. 319), and thus a proper appreciation of communication needs to analyze these oppositions.

An advocate of a strictly quantitative version of content analysis, such as Berelson, is suspicious of any attempt to introduce qualitative considerations into the technique: to do so is to risk its objectivity and systematicness. In fact, Berelson holds that qualitative content analysis is better described as "content assessment," because a subjective and arbitrary valuational component is introduced into the method that results in an unscientific approach differing little from traditional literary textual analysis.

It must be admitted that it is unclear whether qualitative content analysis actually constitutes a distinct technique. It is perhaps more accurately considered a residual category encompassing procedures of coding or interpreting communication content that are at variance with Berelson's strict conception. Kracauer's (1952) definition of qualitative content analysis suggested that it consists of "the selection and rational organization of such categories as condense the substantive meanings of the given text, with a view to testing pertinent assumptions and hypotheses. These categories *may* or *may not* invite frequency counts" (p. 638). Kracauer argued that dependence upon preestablished categories applied to manifest elements of the content of communication can easily result in the inadequate treatment of the significance of key words or phrases; qualitative analysis, in contrast, is appropriately placed to pick up such nuances. Note how far Kracauer's recommendations depart from Berelson's: There is no requirement to treat only manifest content, but equally there are no clear, replicable procedures presented whereby the substantive meanings of a given text can be condensed. Nor are frequency counts barred from qualitative content analysis, but this point simply sidesteps the problem: Under what circumstances is a count to be preferred over a qualitative appraisal of communication content?

These difficulties give some point to Berelson's complaint about the dangers of content assessment once the strict criterion of quantification is abandoned, and it cannot be claimed that Kracauer's conception provides a completely alternative set of principles to guide the investigator. It would be a mistake to dwell upon the quantitative-qualitative debate as here reviewed, however. Many modern content analysts (e.g., Holsti, 1969) simply insist on the requirements of objectivity and systematicness and prefer to treat the issue of manifest or latent content case by case, at the same time insisting on the need to observe replicable scientific procedures. Included in the latter may be some form of measurement, although not necessarily frequency counts: The presence or absence of a theme might be measured, but not the frequency with which it occurs in the data. Second, the arguments for a qualitative content analysis are best read not as recommendations for a *single* alternative technique, but as pointing in the direction of a *range* of methods for analyzing communication content, including those methods that this book addresses in subsequent chapters.

Conclusion

We have reviewed the use of content analysis as a technique to analyze certain social dimensions of fashion. The researchers reported no difficulty in applying the technique to visual data, even though it is most commonly employed to analyze linguistic data. We have also reviewed some of the characteristic strengths and weaknesses of the technique, both of which stem from its quantitative aspect. We conclude the chapter with some remarks on the quantitative-qualitative distinction.

We do not wish to overdraw the distinction between these two very general categories of social scientific research, which are probably better regarded as poles on a continuum rather than in Manichean either/or terms. Quantitative research aims to provide precise, empirically well corroborated statements about the relationship between two or more variables. The values of the variable (e.g., relative deprivation) are represented in numerical form so that measurement can proceed in a quantitative manner and various types of statistical testing can be employed. Qualitative research is not so much interested in the measurement of social variables as it is concerned to investigate the qualities that social phenomena have for the members of a society: the meanings or significance they attribute to beliefs, practices, appearances, types of person, and so forth. Content analysis, as a primarily quantitative method, is not well equipped to give access to those understandings, although as we have shown, it *is* a helpful way of discovering social patterns that operate, as it were, "behind the backs" of society's members and beyond the scope of (some of) their understandings.

The quantitative-qualitative distinction is the methodological dimension of the long-running dispute between proponents of positivism and interpretivism in the social sciences. Although much of what follows will be concerned with interpretivism's contribution to the analysis of visual data, we wish to conclude the chapter, if not on a conciliatory note, at least by cautioning the reader against too easy an acceptance of the convenient dichotomy between quantitative and qualitative research. Qualitative research, let it be noted, does not eschew measurement altogether. Certain actions may be described as occurring "often" or "rarely"; here measurement judgments are made, even though they are not statistically expressed. Quantitative research, for its part, does not rest on solid mathematical bedrock (Cicourel, 1964); there is an irreducible interpretive element in assigning numbers to variables and their indicators. Quantitative and qualitative research are not the opposed extremes they may appear on first sight.

3. SYMBOLIST AND STRUCTURALIST ANALYSES OF VISUAL REPRESENTATIONS

The previous chapter demonstrated the degree to which content analysis is unable to inform us about the qualitative, meaningful dimensions of culture. In the present chapter, we consider two related approaches, symbolic and structuralist analysis, that attempt to address the meaningful aspects of visual representations. We continue the substantive focus of the previous chapter on fashion and the appearance of the human body with a consideration of the Strathems' (1971) symbolist analysis of self-decoration in Mount Hagen, New Guinea, and Lévi-Strauss's (1983) structuralist analysis of Northwest Coast American Indian masks. We conclude with a structuralist analysis of contemporary Western advertising (Williamson, 1978). Throughout, our concern is to outline the general principles of symbolic and structuralist analysis with reference to studies of visual representations.

The Symbolic Meanings of Visual Representations

Let us begin with an elementary point. Visual representations of men's beards, women's dresses, or whatever, reveal what is socially significant to a society's members. Gender, age-grade, class, and race, the so-called master statuses, are often rapidly and effortlessly communicated at a mere glance. And yet the ordinary sense made of appearances is an issue content analysis cannot address, because it fragments naturally occurring meanings, subsuming them under the analyst's categories. In contrast, for investigators working within symbolist and structuralist perspectives, the meanings of these appearances are the keys to a fuller understanding of the culture in which they are embedded. Instead of measuring isolated elements, symbolists and structuralists endeavor to arrive at a fuller appreciation of the visual representation by relating it to other social and cultural arrangements. Thus although symbolists and structuralists agree that the interpretation and use of symbols is a process that is universal to human social life, they differ in the analytic apparatus they employ to investigate that process.

According to one advocate of symbolic anthropology, "The essence of symbolism lies in the recognition of one thing as standing for (re-presenting) another, the relation between them normally being that of concrete to abstract, particular to general" (Firth, 1973, p. 15). A beard may stand for masculinity, or a particular style of dress may represent femininity, respectability, or whatever. The task of the anthropologist is to establish the individual and collective meanings carried by symbols and to explore the logic of their patterning. Meanings operate at several levels. Thus Turner (1967) distinguishes (1) the "exegetical" meaning of a symbol, which derives from indigenous informants; (2) the "operational" meaning, which the anthropologist establishes from observation of the symbol in use; and (3) the "positional" or contextual meaning of a symbol, which derives its relation to other symbols as part of a pattern or system (pp. 50-52). For example, an informant may claim that wearing a beard is simply a matter of individual choice (the exegetical meaning of the beard as a symbol), but the ethnographer may establish that beards are only worn by members of particular social groups, such as priests. From this observation it could be concluded that the operational meaning of the beard is at variance with its exegetical meaning. The positional meaning of the beard requires a more comprehensive analysis. Following Lévi-Strauss, it can be argued that for males beards are the natural condition—nakedness covered by beard growth (attire)—but culture can dictate that nakedness of the face must be revealed.

Symbols are made sense of by reference to other symbols. The graphic symbols Δ and O represent male and female in anthropological kinship diagrams, but an explanation of the graphic symbols takes place through language, the major symbolic system in human cultures. Within a society, symbols may cluster together as codes, such as fashion, gender, and so forth. The interpretation of a symbol—establishing what it "stands for"—is sometimes problematic, as symbols are essentially polysemic, i.e., they may represent several things. For instance, in Asia the swastika, 卍 , is a religious symbol that means something quite different from the political associations it has in Europe. The ethnographer's task of decoding symbolism is complicated by the polysemy of symbols, a difficulty formulated in the Lévi-Straussian observation that everything is meaningful but nothing is meant. This suggests both the ambiguity that inheres in symbols and the interpretive latitude open to viewers and hearers.

As Firth (1973) observed, "Symbolization is a universal human process" (p. 15). The social world is symbolically constituted and mediated. Actions, appearances, and artifacts all carry symbolic significance; greetings, hair-styles, beards, dress styles, and flags may all symbolize socially meaningful matters. It is therefore not surprising to find that a range of academic disciplines, including art history, literary criticism, philosophy, psychology, and theology, have addressed issues arising out of symbolism. Anthropological interest has focused on the use of symbols within cultures, and some anthropologists contend with Firth that this provides a major "key to the understanding of social structure and social process" (p. 25). We examine this claim with respect to two anthropological studies and one sociological study.

A Symbolist Analysis of Self-Decoration

Self-Decoration in Mount Hagen (Strathern & Strathern, 1971) examines ceremonial adornment of men and women in a remote area of the New Guinea highlands. Self-decoration involves face painting, oiling the body, and wearing specialized items of clothing and adornment such as shells, plumes, leaves, grasses, furs, wigs, aprons, bones, and drums. Some of these items are valuable and function as exchangeable commodities in the *moka,* the central ritual in the ceremonial life of Hagen. Since there is no hereditary position of chief and no overt hierarchical relations, the leaders of groups in Hagen ("big men") continually compete with each other. Hageners produce sufficient food surpluses to enable them to engage in quite elaborate ceremonies, religious cult activities, and economic exchanges. As the Stratherns suggest,

> Periodic displays and gifts of wealth mediate relations between big men and between clans, highlighting both links and rivalries. It is at these displays that formal sets of decorations are worn. What decorations the participants actually wear is partly a result of big men's pronouncements, but it also depends on individual effort and choice. (pp. 16-17)

Self-decoration is employed on both informal and formal occasions. Hageners decorate themselves informally for daily life, roadworking (Strathern & Strathern, 1971, plates 27 and 28), courting parties (Plate 22), and extraordinarily, for warfare. Formal situations include religious cult performances and *moka* ceremonies (Color Plate 4; see Figure 3.1). When individuals employ self-decoration informally, they symbolically reveal

Figure 3.1. Donors at a Kuli festival make their *kanan*-dance entry, distinguished by feather plaques above the black Enga-style wigs. Photo from Strathern & Strathern.

various aspects of themselves, whereas the formal situations assert collective aspects of culture such as group prosperity and lineage ties.

Much of the book is devoted to a detailed description of the varieties of self-decoration, the methods of making decorations, the sources of decorative materials in the environment, the occasions upon which certain forms of self-decoration are appropriate, and the symbolism associated with particular colors. Two aspects of the Stratherns' work are selected for consideration here: the role of self-decoration on formal occasions as an "epideictic display" and the symbolism of color and face painting. In characterizing decorations as epideictic displays, the authors suggest that particular qualities of the item of decoration may transfer to the wearer:

> Just as spells call on things and harness them by the power of words (through metaphor), so the actual wearing of items of decoration can magically promote the wearer's desires (by metonymy—they become as strong or attractive as the birds of prey or the kilt tree by donning a part taken from them). Men will thus be as powerful as the things they wear. (1971, p. 138)

Herein lies the importance of the painstaking work of identifying the material components of self-decoration, for they are replete with symbolic significance.

Thus, Hagener attire comprises an assembly of symbolic items which, whole or in part, visually imbue the wearers with the magic and energy of the items worn. The magic of the symbols is visually transferred, involving association and mimesis; the symbolic items are believed to imbue the wearer with the magic that inheres in them. Wearers acquire the symbolic energy of the items worn, which visually become a part of them (the iridescence of the shells, the magnificence of bird of paradise plumes, or whatever); via visual mimesis, they become what they wear. Consider, for example, the array of symbolic items used for self-decoration in Figure 3.1, captioned "Donors at a Kuli festival." The items include pearl shell crescents, plumage kilts, wigs, leaves and grasses, etc., indicating clearly how symbols are embedded in and made sense of by reference to other symbols.

The high quality of the Stratherns' descriptive work is also in evidence in the chapters on face painting and the connotations of color. Our interest is in the relation of text to the visual data (photographs, diagrams), for the book is a richly illustrated volume containing 115 photographs and 26 line drawings. The line drawings serve to visually identify the different types of face design; they are complemented by the verbal terms Hageners employ to describe these designs: The charcoal-darkened, typically male face "cut" by a white line (*kaklpa pokla ronom*) is shown in a photograph (1971, Plate 67; see Figure 3.2). Snake-skin paint—a design featuring chevrons and interlocking diamonds and *waep kerua* (Line Diagram Figures 2 and 3c; our Figure 3.2)—can be employed by both young unbearded males (Plate 71; see Figure 3.3) and, more commonly, women (Plate 69; see Figure 3.4). By closely integrating careful ethnographic description with the visual data, the authors are able to discern the elements of face painting and indicate the gender codes they symbolize.

The symbolism of color occupies a central place in the analysis of face painting in particular and self-decoration in general. Color has a distinct comparative significance in the study of self-decoration. In most cultures, color is replete with symbolic significance. In both self-decoration and other symbolic systems, colors and color preferences can distinguish different categories of persons, for instance males and females. In order to explore the symbolic meaning and significance of colors and color combination to Hageners, the Stratherns elicited and observed folk conceptions of color and their culturally appropriate use. From this manifest data, the Stratherns constructed abstract, latent models of color significance, proposing the following overall associations:

RED	WHITE	BLACK
Brightness: fertility, attractiveness		Darkness: disguise, aggressiveness
Female (+ male) associations	Predominantly male associations	Male associations

TABLE 3.1

SOURCE: Strathern and Strathern, 1971, p. 158

This table indicates that for the Hageners, certain combinations of dark (with limited bright) colors on faces have male associations, whereas a predominance of generally bright and attractive colors tend to have female associations. By focusing on colors in face painting, it becomes clear that

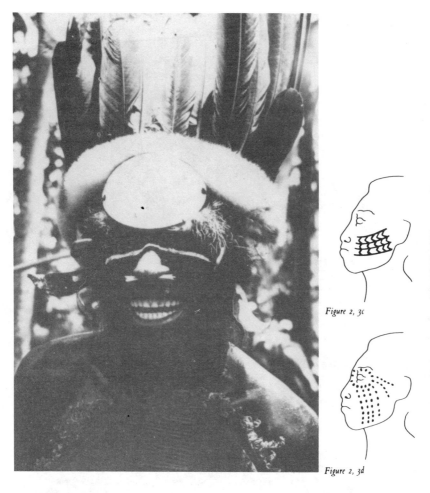

Figure 2, 3c

Figure 2, 3d

Figure 3.2. The face "cut" by a white line. Photo from Strathern & Strathern.

different combinations of designs with their respective colors convey quite different symbolic messages. For example, in Figure 3.2 the charcoal darkened male face is cut with a white line that symbolically conveys adult maleness, whereas the facial decoration in Figure 3.3, in combination with other items of self-decoration, symbolizes that this is a young not yet fully

Figure 3.3. Although wearing *koi wal*, this unbearded lad has his face painted like a girl's. Photo from Strathern & Strathern.

adult male; the design is also used by women, as in Figure 3.4. Generally, however, women's faces are brighter and more "attractive," as shown in

Figure 3.4. Girls dancing with men, cheeks brightly adorned with chevrons (right) and Lozenges (left). Photo from Strathern & Strathern.

the Stratherns' Color Plate 19 (1971, following p. 164), which indicates extensive use of red, blue, and white face paints (a point that cannot be conveyed in black-and-white photography). Self-decoration is thus a visual medium for communicating symbolic information, and as the Stratherns argue, "An examination of the details of decoration will show us, further, that a whole battery of messages can be transmitted through different combinations of items" (p. 59). This indicates both the highly symbolic quality of self-decoration and also the complex of informational combinations and possibilities available in a visual medium.

At the formal level, the general functions of Hagen self-decoration are to prepare the person for participation at an exchange festival, to encourage the development of an emotional state appropriate to that participation, and to demonstrate socially valued abstract and ideal qualities (Strathern & Strathern, 1971, pp. 171-172). At a deeper level (the "positional" meaning of self-decoration), the Stratherns suggest that the balance of brightness and darkness symbolizes friendship between clans and rivalry between them, or the "feminine" values of fertility and friendly relations versus the "masculine" values of strength and aggressiveness. These analytic claims are very much the product of the carefully crafted and detailed ethnographic account the Stratherns provide of Hagen symbolism. As already indicated, however, symbols are open to a multiplicity of meanings, and as the Stratherns observe, certain of the items apparently have no explicit "meaning." "It is just decoration," the wearers say (1971, dust jacket).

Structuralism

Contemporary structuralism owes its origins to the Swiss linguist Saussure. The basic unit of language is the sign, according to Saussure, and language is a system of signs in which words are only "arbitrarily" tied to meanings. There is no necessary link between a "sound-image" (Saussure, 1959, p. 16) such as "table" (the *signifier*) and the concept or meaning (the *signified*) of this particular sound-image (a flat-surfaced object). The link between signifier and signified is established purely through the conventions of language. Thus, the meaning of any sign results from the conventions that connect signifier and signified.

Of central importance for Saussure were the ways in which signs are related together in a language. He identified two dimensions of these relations: syntagmatic and paradigmatic relations. *Syntagmatic relations* concern the sequential arrangement of words in an utterance or sentence (the meaning of "the cat sat on the mat" unfolds over the course of its statement). *Paradigmatic relations* concern the "vertical" arrangement between signs: the choice between "napped" or "stood" as alternatives to "sat" in the previous example. Language is thus a self-defining and self-regulating system of signs, and the meanings of signs reside in the system of categorical relations and differences established within the language, not in the relation of signs to external reality.

Saussure identified two dimensions of language, *langue* and *parole,* which correspond to language in its abstract form ("the English language") and the speech that occurs in everyday situations. *Langue* underlies and determines every manifestation of *parole* in the world, and yet it has no concrete existence in itself. If *parole* is considered on its own, it appears to lack coherence or pattern; but fragments of ordinary talk are coherent and patterned, a consequence of their structuring by *langue.*

Modern structuralism has generalized this distinction beyond linguistics and has sought to uncover the *langue* underlying the *parole* of a variety of cultural arrangements, such as kinship, totemism, mythology, advertising, and funeral work (Manning, 1987; Barley, 1983a, 1983b). Investigators seek the hidden or deeper "structures," "codes," and "grammars" that under-pin empirical phenomena. For instance, in Lévi-Strauss's (1969) *Elementary Structures of Kinship,* the Maussian notion of reciprocity, *give* and *take,* is the deeper structure found to be common to all kinship systems (Lévi-Strauss, 1969; Mauss, 1966). Lévi-Strauss's structuralism thus promotes a data-sensitive, cognitively oriented mode of analysis, in which empirical phenomena are skillfully reduced to a series of binary oppositions that underlie them; for example, in the case of myths, *nature* versus *culture.* The oppositional models produced indicate the structural frameworks within which thought is done, its basic conceptual parameters. We develop certain of these ideas further by considering Lévi-Strauss's (1983) *Way of the Masks* and Williamson's (1978) *Decoding Advertisements.*

The "Voice" of the Masks

Lévi-Strauss's analysis of American Northwest Coast Indian masks is, like the Stratherns' study, an investigation of symbolism, but it departs from the latter by being conducted from a distinctly structuralist vantage. The Stratherns' analysis was based on detailed ethnographic work within a single culture, but Lévi-Strauss investigated three related American Indian groups, the Kwakiutl, the Salish, and the Haida. These provide the necessary com-parative basis for the identification of the abstract structures underlying the empirical manifestations of mask styles. A further point of contrast is that although the Stratherns' study was located in the ethnographic present, Lévi-Strauss analyzed the use of masks during the nineteenth and early twentieth centuries, in cultures that are in no substantial sense presently operational. The Stratherns relied upon their fieldwork observations as sources of data. Lévi-Strauss drew on secondary sources to explore a dis-tinctly visual aspect of American Indian culture, the ritual and symbolic use of masks. Masks evidently differ from self-decoration; they are what the Stratherns termed representational, insofar as they figuratively and some would argue literally transform the wearer into another person, animal, bird, fish, spirit, or whatever (Walens, 1981).

Lévi-Strauss commenced his book in a characteristically ebullient manner, evoking the magic these mask styles held for him. He noted his admiration for their aesthetic properties even as he indicated the analytical problem they posed:

> Looking at these masks, I was ceaselessly asking myself the same questions. Why this unusual shape, so ill-adapted to their function? Of course I was seeing them incomplete because in the old days they were topped by a crown of swan or golden eagle feathers . . . intermingled with some thin reeds adorned by "snowballs" of down that quivered with every movement of the wearer. . . . But these trimmings, which may be seen in old photographs, rather accentuate the strongness of the mask without shedding any light on its mysterious aspects: why the gaping mouth, the flabby lower jaw exhibiting an enormous tongue? Why the birds' heads, which have no obvious connection with the rest and are most incongruously placed? Why the protruding eyes, which are the unvarying trait of all the types? Finally, why the quasi-demonic style resembling nothing else in the neighbouring cultures, or even in the culture which gave it birth? (1983, p. 12)

Lévi-Strauss's strikingly visual problem was, Why should a mask of this people look like this, be constructed in this manner, adopt this plastic form—why *this?* He fashioned his solution from a structural analysis of the myths, particularly myths of ancestry and origin, decoding the visual styles and symbolism of the masks by recourse to the stories embodied in cultural mythology. Lévi-Strauss's ingenious solution uses cultural knowledge in the form of words, myths, to analytically explore masks, distinctly visual artifacts. In certain key respects, this transformation from the palpable visual domain of artifacts to the realm of words and myths is less startling than it might initially seem, particularly when the original French title of the book is considered, *La Voie des Masques.* In French, *voie* (way) is a homophone of *voix* (voice), which implies that masks have voices (Modelski, 1983). In Lévi-Strauss's analysis masks, apparently inert artifacts accessible to us in the visual mode, are regarded as "talking" to us, and their messages are embedded in cultural mythology, masks as good to think with. In a "discipline of words," Lévi-Strauss's strikingly visual problem is solved by recourse to the narrative of myths, which have the cognitive power to explain away the problem.

The first chapter is titled "Enigma of *a* Mask" (our emphasis). For Lévi-Strauss, variations on a single mask style remained an enigma until compared to other related masks and their associated mythologies. Lévi-Strauss's analysis is data sensitive in that it addresses individual manifestations of phenomena. This individuality is apprehended by locating a particular mask style in the context of related styles, so that similarities and differences are visually available. The particulars of an individual mask style thus make structural sense when seen in contrast and comparison with related styles. Lévi-Strauss's visual problem—the enigma of a mask—is explored structurally, following his hypothesis that masks like myths embody more than their immediate appearances and visually echo what they transform.

Using myths as evidence, Lévi-Strauss then compared two related styles of masks, which comprise stylistic variants of his enigma, the Swaihwé masks of the Salish and the Xwéxwé masks of the neighboring Kwakiutl (Lévi-Strauss, 1983, following p. 92; figures 3.5 and 3.6). The two mask styles share certain externalized visual plastic features: cylinder eyes, a lolling tongue, birdlike dimensions, and so forth. Although at the purely visual level the masks look similar, at the social level they contextually serve very different purposes in potlatch wealth-dispensing ceremonies, at which coppers and other items of prestige are given and received—The Swaihwé masks are used to dispense wealth, and the Xwéxwé to withhold. Visually similar masks thus serve distinct purposes in different cultural contexts: For the Salish, the mask style symbolizes giving, whereas for the Kwakiutl the mask style symbolizes withholding. Among certain of the Kwakiutl there is, however, another radically different style of mask that is used to dispense wealth, the Dzonokwa. Visually Dzonokwa is an almost perfect inversion of the Swaihwé and Xwéxwé styles (Lévi-Strauss, 1983, following p. 92; Figure 3.7). The Dzonokwa mask exhibits hollow sunken cheeks and eye sockets, a minimal mouth with round, pursed lips, and minimal ears and nose, often surrounded by dark fur or hair. In terms of its plastic form, the significant point is that the emphasis is on minimum features rather than maximum features, and externalization rather than internalization, a transformation of the visual oppositions, *external-internal* and *maximum-minimum*.

When Swaihwé and Dzonokwa masks are compared, "The two complement each other almost like a mould and its cast" (Lévi-Strauss, 1983, p. 67). Salish myths emphasize the origin of Swaihwé masks *inside* culture, suggesting that in ancestral times the images dropped from the sky above or arose from the waters below. In contrast, the Dzonokwa mask symbolizes a mythical ogress of supernatural powers who resides *outside* of culture in nature, in the forests and mountains afar, the wilderness (Lévi-Strauss, 1983; Duerr, 1985).

Figure 3.5. Swaihwé mask.

Figure 3.6. Xwéxwé mask.

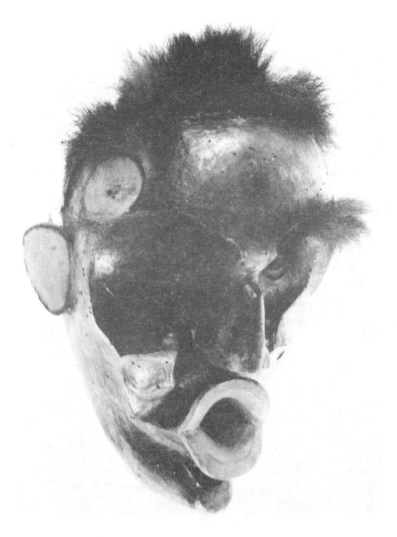

Figure 3.7. Dzonokwa mask.

Schematically, Dzonokwa masks arguably relate to Swaihwé and Xwéxwé masks in the following structural transformational manner:

	Salish	*Kwakiutl*	
	Swaihwé	Xwéxwé	Dzonokwa
Relationship to Wealth	dispense	withhold	dispense
Visual Features *(Traits Plastiques)*	external	external	internal
Social Relationships	inside (culture)	inside (culture)	outside (nature)

TABLE 3.2

To conclude, it is notable that although the origins and social relationships of the masks and their use arise from the analysis of mythical data, and require to be thought about conceptually, the *traits plastique* of the masks' external and internal transformations are visually available and seeable symbolic structures that can only be known through visual examination and analysis.

Lévi-Strauss must have the last word:

> I hope to have shown that a mask is not primarily what it represents but what it transforms, that is to say, what it chooses not to represent. Like a myth, a mask denies as much as it affirms. It is not made solely of what it says or thinks it is saying, but of what it excludes. (1983, p. 144)

Decoding Advertisements

Williamson's (1978) widely admired analysis of advertising imagery can also be described as structuralist, although in her case the major intellectual influences are Althusserian Marxism and Barthes's semiotics. Consequently the major themes of Williamson's book are the ideologies constructed by advertising and the devices used by particular advertisements to convey their meaning. Her interest resides in "what can be *seen* in advertisements" (p. 11), and she maintains, "We can only understand what advertisements mean by finding out *how* they mean, and analysing the way in which they work" (p. 17).

For Williamson, advertisements are assemblages of signs that produce the meanings that help to sell products and thus to promote consumerist ideologies. As noted earlier, a sign consists of two elements, the signifier (the material object, word, or picture) and the signified (the meaning ascribed to the material object, word, or picture). Hence the structuralist slogan: A sign is always thing-plus-meaning.

The skillful application of this basic principle reveals how particular advertisements work to convey their meanings. Let us consider three perfume advertisements analyzed by Williamson (1978, plates A8, A9, A55; our figures 3.8, 3.9 and 3.10). The first shows a bottle of Chanel No. 5 set against the background of Catherine Deneuve's face (Figure 3.8). In small type, we read "Catherine Deneuve for Chanel." This is an example of an advertisement that operates by *correlative sign-work,* i.e., the simple juxtaposition of the product and Catherine Deneuve. The meanings we associate with Catherine Deneuve (French sophistication, glamour, beauty) are transferred to the product. Williamson writes that this advertisement is

> appropriating a relationship that exists in that system between signifier (Catherine Deneuve) and signified (glamour, beauty) to speak of its products in terms of the same relationship; so that the perfume can be substituted for Catherine Deneuve's face and can also be made to signify glamour and beauty. (1978, p. 25)

Catherine Deneuve is part of a wider set or collection of signifiers, including various public personalities, such as models and film stars. The sense of "French chic" we associate with Catherine Deneuve arises because the referent system is a system of differences. That is, the particular meaning of French chic that Catherine Deneuve's face has for us arises from what she is not compared to other analogous signs in the film star/modeling system, such as Margaux Hemingway (see Figure 3.9). The signifier Margaux Hemingway practicing karate yields a very different signified (youthfulness, exuberance, assertiveness). But importantly for Williamson, these meanings do not simply arise from what is palpably evident in the advertisement. The advertisement "itself depends for its significance on not being Catherine Deneuve's image" (1978, p. 27). The contrast between the products Chanel No. 5 and Babe is made by the social contrast ("feminine" vs. "liberated") that is signified by Catherine Deneuve and Margaux Hemingway. For Williamson, this is the "logic" of these advertisements: Catherine Deneuve is to Margaux

Figure 3.8. Catherine Deneuve for Chanel. Photo from Williamson.

Figure 3.9. Margaux Hemingway and Babe. Photo from Williamson.

Figure 3.10. Chanel No. 5 ad. Photo from Williamson.

Hemingway as Chanel No. 5 is to Babe. And this is how differing products develop the associations they have in the minds of consumers.

Another technique used to convey an advertising image is for the product itself to act as signified, as in the Chanel No. 5 advertisement (Williamson, 1978, Plate A55; Figure 3.10). Williamson writes: "This is pure advertisement: the very essence of all advertising" (p. 90). The advertisement is a sign that is also attempting to present its referent, real bottles of Chanel No. 5, which of course are absent. Hence the peculiar "transparency" of this advertisement.

Williamson examined a further range of techniques that advertisements employ to convey their message. Of particular interest is the mirror image technique. A model is depicted looking back at the viewer in the same manner that we see our image in a mirror (e.g., 1978, Plate A34). What is signified by this technique is an identificatory process: You too can become like the image in the advertisement if you use the product. The mirror technique is one method of facilitating our involvement in the advertisement, but there are also others in common use. Viewer involvement can be generated by the skillful use of "absence" where, for example, the advertisement implies an absent person outside the advertisement itself (see Plate A41; our Figure 3.11). The woman's utterance is a reply to a question about what she would like to drink, implying that she is responding to a man who is not pictured. Viewer involvement is also created by irony, puns, and puzzles, as in the More cigarette advertisement (Plate A52); the caption reads, "If you aren't getting More, you're getting less."

The other focus of Williamson's analysis addresses the major *referent systems* employed in contemporary advertising. In reading and viewing advertisements, the knowledge of the viewer is brought to bear. It is this knowledge, these systems of meanings, that are *referred to* by advertisements (1978, p. 95). Williamson again uses structuralist concepts to analyze this body of knowledge.

"Nature" is one referent system widely employed in advertisements. Images of nature are commonplace and the connotations of "goodness" and "wholesomeness" unashamedly exploited. So too is the metaphor of the "cooking" of nature (see Bird's Eye orange juice, Williamson, 1978, Plate A62). Magical referent systems are also employed. Here the product appears to result from a disproportionately minimal investment of effort (e.g., the astounding results of drinking a certain brand of vodka). A third referent system is "time"; images of the past draw on nostalgic connotations whilst those of the future appear to promise exaggerated possibilities for future

Figure 3.11. Dry Sack ad. Photo from Williamson.

generations of consumers, in a combination of the magic referent system and the frequent deployment of science to tame or "cook" nature.

The first part of Williamson's study thus attempts to uncover the interior logic of the advertisements. The second part considers what the viewer brings to the visual image. In structuralist terminology, we are presented with an analysis of both the *encoding* and the *decoding* of one class of visual imagery, the advertisement.

Conclusion

The current chapter has indicated how symbolic and structuralist analyses can be applied with penetrating results to visual materials such as self-decoration, masks, and advertisements. Each of the works considered exhibits its own distinguishing characteristics. The Stratherns' book is rich in ethnographic detail, including some 115 photographs, and involved a light application of theory. In contrast, the work of both Lévi-Strauss and Williamson is less ethnographically detailed, but more reliant on preconceived theoretical ideas. The relative balance between ethnographic detail and theoretical explanation affords an array of attendant analytical advantages and disadvantages. Ethnographers are often rightly suspicious of "over-theorized" texts, and Lévi-Strauss's and Williamson's studies occasionally verge on this, stretching the reader's credibility (see Williamson's analysis of the MG advertisement, 1978, p. 121, Plate A73, for one example).

Lévi-Strauss observed about the works of Radin, which he uses as data, "A crop harvested by Paul Radin, even if he should not choose to mill the grain himself, is always capable of providing lasting nourishment for many generations of students" (1978, p. 198). Similarly, we anticipate that the Stratherns' book on self-decoration will provide a fertile source of ethnographic materials for future generations of scholars seeking to explore the visual aspects of culture.

4. THE SOCIAL ORGANIZATION OF VISUAL EXPERIENCE

In this last chapter, we consider what cognitive anthropology and ethnomethodology may have to offer the analysis of the seen world. We also develop some previously introduced themes by briefly considering anthropological postmodernism. The central concern of the chapter is the social organization of visual experience: the idea that people's experience of the seen world is culturally shaped and socially constituted and mediated.

Schutz's (1967) phenomenological thinking about intersubjectivity and Goffman's (1974) frame analysis are two influential schemes suggesting that human experience is socially organized. The difficulty with both schemes lies in their utilization as systematic empirical methods. Schutz's orientation is essentially philosophical, although his work has been an important influence on the development of ethnomethodology, a decidedly empirical approach; Goffman's work, tied as it is so closely to the ingenuity of its author, has proved difficult to apply in a systematic manner. For these reasons, in this chapter, we examine two approaches that do offer guidelines for systematic ethnographic studies of visual experience: cognitive anthropology and ethnomethodology.

Experience as it occurs in the visual field is always of something (Husserl, 1970, 1973), and it may encompass more than the material objects of the seen world. It can include abstract phenomena like music, mathematics, philosophy, physics, pain, emotions, and memories (Coulter, 1979, 1989). Our interest in visual experience thus encompasses what is seen, and is socially recognized, classified, and organized as seen, irrespective of philosophical questions of independent existence. In short, to be concerned analytically with experience is to treat seriously what people are aware of and notice as part of their everyday world. Cognitive anthropology shares with ethnomethodology this general concern with the social organization of experience, and we shall consider how it treats visual experience.

Our concern in this chapter is thus with the ways in which "natives" (as Geertz [1976] would say "in the strict sense of the term"—i.e., to universally denote cultural members) order their experience of the seen world. Cognitive anthropology and ethnomethodology share a common empirical focus, treating natives' (members') concerns, beliefs, and practices as ethnographic data. The ordinary everyday understandings held by natives about their experience, conduct, and thought is a common analytical orientation of both approaches, although they differ markedly in the manner in which the inquiry is conducted and the theories that subtly guide them. For cognitive anthropology, it is some version of the Sapir-Whorf theory of linguistic relativism, and for ethnomethodology, Wittgenstein's later ideas about language and Schutz's attempt to phenomenologically ground interpretive sociology.

In common with the structuralism of Lévi-Strauss and Williamson, cognitive anthropology and ethnomethodology orient to the cognitive dimension in a data-sensitive manner. Differences between structuralism and the perspectives considered in this chapter are evident, however, at the analytical and methodological levels. The analytical differences can be summarized in Geertz's (1976) well-known distinction: Structuralist models tend to be "experience distant," whereas those of cognitive anthropology and ethnomethodology tend to be "experience near." Admittedly, this is only an approximation, as the more abstract and technical analyses of the latter perspectives tend to gravitate toward the experience-distant pole. But whereas structuralism views beliefs, experience, and so on as simply manifestations of deeper structures, cognitive anthropology and ethnomethodology maintain that there is an investigable social organization evident in the expression of beliefs and people's ordinary experience. Thus, methodologically, both cognitive anthropology and ethnomethodology characteristically rely on ethnographically collected data of actual human conduct as the basis for their investigations of the social organization of experience, and additionally, ethnomethodology is sensitive to the reflexive construction of what passes as data in the ethnographic research setting. In contrast, Lévi-Strauss's work is founded primarily on the analysis of previously collected materials.

Cognitive anthropology and ethnomethodology share a common concern to display a disciplined stance toward fundamental issues of ethnographic description, known as displaying ethnoscience in cognitive anthropology and doing rigorous description in ethnomethodology. Although cognitive anthropology's attempts to promote an ethnoscience generate in part what Geertz (1973) termed "thin descriptions," ethnomethodology's phenomenological products frequently facilitate a "thicker" description. The extent to which cognitive anthropology and ethnomethodology attempt to incorporate respectively scientific rigor and phenomenological sensitivity into their descriptive apparatuses are matters we address in our treatment of how they explore the social organization of visual experience.

Cognitive Anthropology

Cognitive anthropology has been referred to variously as ethnosemantics, ethnoscience, technical ethnography, and taxonomic, componential, or domain analysis. Ethnosemantics offers a distinctive view of the nature of culture and the task of ethnographic description. As Frake (1969) suggests, it is concerned with "discerning how people construe their world of experience from the way they talk about it" (p. 29). It regards culture as constituting a vital cognitive dimension: Culture is not to be regarded as simply people, things, behavior, and emotions, but includes a cognitive reference to the *knowledge* and *beliefs* that natives hold about specifiable categories of people, things, behavior, and emotions. In Goodenough's (1957) classic definition, "A society's culture consists of whatever it is one has to know or believe in order to operate in a manner acceptable to its members, and do so in any role that they accept for any one of themselves" (p. 167). The task of ethnographic description is thus the specification of the knowledge and beliefs necessary for an individual to operate acceptably in the group under investigation. Thus, the test of the adequacy of the description is the extent to which it furnishes a basis for a stranger to be sufficiently well culturally equipped to act appropriately within the society.

The native's cultural competence is the focus of ethnosemantic investigation. It is assumed that in order to communicate within a culture, people must categorize the world in much the same way; these categories are encoded in the semantic system of the language. Cultural competence can be approached through the medium of the native's ordinary usage of vernacular terms. Within any sphere of life, or "cultural domain," a system of categories can be uncovered or "elicited" and the organized features of the system presented as a "taxonomy." Thus a color taxonomy presents the culture's terms for categorizing the color of objects; a kinship taxonomy will identify the relevant terms for family members and relations among them. In principle, the knowledge and beliefs required for appropriate behavior in *any* cultural domain can be elicited; as in, for example, the knowledge and beliefs needed to work as a cocktail waitress in a college bar in the United States (Spradley & Mann, 1975).

Ethnosemantics, like ethnomethodology, marks a break within the ethnographic tradition that was content to construct its descriptions out of the analytical terminology of its parent discipline (e.g., agnatic lineage systems; work alienation). Instead, culture is to be approached through the concepts and classifications of its natives. This is sometimes described as a shift from "etic" to "emic" concerns (Pike, 1954) and expresses an analytical stance of respect toward the native's own experience. Of course, that experience cannot be fully captured by ethnosemantic methods, as Frake (1969) acknowledged:

> The analysis of a culture's terminological systems will not . . . exhaustively reveal the cognitive world of its members, but it will certainly tap a central portion of it. Culturally significant cognitive features must be communicable between persons in one of the standard symbolic systems of the culture. A

major share of these features will undoubtedly be codable in a society's most flexible and productive communicative device, its language. Evidence tends to suggest that those cognitive features requiring most frequent communication will tend to have standard and relatively short linguistic labels. (p. 30)

Thus, to give the standard example, the significance of snow to Eskimos is conveyed in the 25 or so terms they employ in their vocabulary. Analysis of ordinary language can thus provide indicators of culturally significant aspects of cognition.

The core of ethnosemantic analysis involves collecting together the culturally significant categories and spelling out the relations between them. This task is facilitated by a number of techniques, including semantic domain analysis, paradigm analysis, genealogy construction, and componential analysis, all of which are variants of taxonomic analysis. (For an instruction manual that breaks down the elements of ethnosemantic research into clearly defined steps—a "developmental research sequence"—see Spradley, 1980.)

Color Terminology

Color is an essential feature of the seen world. Objects are experienced, classified, and described using their color as a significant identificatory principle. In English, there are red bricks, green trees, black gates, white people, yellow taxis, blue flowers, etc. Colors are of course also metaphorized such that an individual can be described as green (naive or raw), blue (melancholy, depressed), red (socialist/marxist or angry), etc. For people everywhere, seen objects exhibit colors in varying degrees. Even though individual perceptions may vary, and there exists the clinical condition of color blindness, most cultures have standardized lexical terminologies or models for indexing color-relevant matters. Sometimes, however, as with the Hanunoo, the culture may lack a word that can be judged for practical purposes equivalent to the English term color (Conklin, 1955). For the Hanunoo, color terms also include much non-color-relevant information concerning, for example, the object's texture, whereas in general English usage, a color exhibits only the "basic" dimensions of brightness, saturation, and hue. Thus an analysis of ordinary language can provide an appropriate avenue to investigate the mental sets natives routinely employ to categorize the seen world in color terms.

There is a long tradition of comparative anthropological investigations of symbolic color use, including the works of Rivers (1901), Evans-Pritchard (1940), and Turner (1967). Color terminologies have been extensively investigated by ethnosemantics (see Berlin & Kay, 1969). The classic consideration is Conklin's (1955) investigation of Hanunoo color categories that developed from his broader interest in Hanunoo ethnobotany. His theoretical departure point is Sapir-Whorf's position of cultural relativism. He briefly outlines technical scientific treatments of color systems, arguing, "Under laboratory conditions, color discrimination is probably the same for all human populations, irrespective of language; but the manner in which languages classify the millions of 'colors' which every normal individual can discriminate differ" (p. 340). Conklin used general ethnographic techniques in his investigation. He elicited color responses from the Hanunoo by showing them combinations of painted cards, dyed fabrics, and other items collected from their cultural and natural environment. From these investigations he concluded that among the Hanunoo, "Much attention is paid to the texture of the surface referred to, the resulting degree and type of reflection (iridescent, sparkling, dull) and to admixture of other nonformal qualities. Frequently these noncolorimetric aspects are considered of primary importance, the more spectrally-definable qualities serving only as secondary attributes" (p. 343). For Conklin, Hanunoo color categories are organized by distinctions made at two major levels of contrast, and he develops a componential analysis of his four level-one terms. The distinctions are associated with brightness, darkness, wetness, and dryness. Color is sui generis visual, but nowhere in Conklin's or most other ethnosemantic works are readers presented with visual representations of the colors discussed.

Probably the most elaborate ethnosemantically influenced work to consider color is Berlin and Kay (1969). The book runs counter to the established Sapir-Whorf orthodoxy of much cognitive anthropology, by proposing that universals can be identified concerning the range of color terms employed in human societies and the evolutionary sequence in which the categories develop. In one sense, they take seriously Conklin's suggestion that color discrimination is probably identical for all human populations. Berlin and Kay's major conclusion is that for humans there are exactly 11 basic color categories: white, black, red, yellow, green, blue, brown, gray, purple, pink, and orange, and these "serve as the psychophysical referents of the eleven or fewer basic color terms in any language" (p. 104).

Ethnoscience

As noted earlier, an alternative title for cognitive anthropology is ethnoscience, and this characterization conveys certain core ideas of the approach.

Following certain orientations in linguistics, cognitive anthropology has placed great emphasis on demonstrating "scientific" rigor in the collection and analysis of its ethnographic materials. This is to be contrasted with what it implicitly regards as the "softer," less disciplined and less scientific orientations of other ethnographic approaches. With the development of contemporary paradigms, cognitive anthropology's expressed desire to be scientific opens its analysis to criticisms emanating from anthropological postmodernism.

Science is the core of modernism, and scientific representations of nature and culture are founded essentially on a visualist epistemology; science is regarded as the mirror of nature (Rorty, 1979). As advocates of postmodernism never tire of informing us, science operates a form of alchemy in which subjects are split from the objects of their inquiry (Fabian, 1983; Clifford & Marcus, 1986; Marcus & Fischer, 1986). Science characterizes and encases its objects in a detached, authoritative language, thereby enacting the Cartesian split (Husserl, 1960). For postmodernism, science is an investigative stricture that separates objects of inquiry from the subjects experiencing them.

This split is graphically evident in the products of cognitive anthropology. Collections of native categories are presented as though inherent in them is a taxonomic organization. This conceptual filtering attempts to retain and show the cogency of the natives' terminological logic, while suggesting its scientific qualities. This logic presumably attempts to mirror nature, for example, the Eskimos' 25 or so terms for snow is a far more elaborate semantic mirror than most European vocabularies allow. Ironically, Stephen Tyler, one of cognitive anthropology's early proponents, is now in the position of analytically exorcising his ethnoscientific past in calling for a postmodern ethnography (Tyler, 1969; 1986).

The analyst's knife is inserted into nature, the whole, to initially sever it from culture, and then by continuing subdivision, the experiencing subject is split from its objects. These discriminations are made according to the dictates of scientific rationality and inquiry. The very methodicity of science hinges on the increasing sophistication and penetration of the scientific analytical gaze: Matter becomes thought of as molecules, atoms, quarks, etc., a taxonomy of continuing division and subdivision. Similarly within cognitive anthropology, after eliciting natives' categories, the analyst's knife dissects and arranges them into a collection of discrete objects, which are presented as exhibiting a taxonomic relation one to the other. An initial respect for the natives' viewpoint recedes into the distance as the analyst's commitment to the norms of scientific rationality, evident in the construction of taxonomies, becomes manifest.

As a form of representation, the language of science uses a powerful visualist epistemology that is evocatively interwoven with visual imagery and root metaphors. The visualist dimension of scientific representation is literally visually available in the ethnoscientific analysis, particularly in its use of graphic taxonomic representations that show hierarchy, division, subdivision, contrast, and relations of inclusion and exclusion of categories. When presented in diagram form, the relational properties of the terminological system are available at a glance, showing the native's cognitive map.

Ethnomethodology

Ethnomethodology is the study of the methods people use for making sense of their everyday experience. In common with cognitive anthropology, it takes seriously the native's point of view. The two approaches also share a cognitive or experiential notion of culture, but ethnomethodology differs markedly in its reflexive sensitivity to its data and in the manner in which it analytically explores the data. Ethnomethodology is critical of cognitive anthropology, arguing that it cannot meet its own test of adequacy—its taxonomic models are not sufficiently detailed and sensitive to actual social contexts to permit a cultural stranger to behave appropriately (Wieder, 1971; Coulter, 1973; Eglin, 1980). Accordingly, ethnomethodology advocates the close investigation of actual courses of social action rather than, as in cognitive anthropology, attempting to produce rulelike characterizations of cultural terminologies.

How, then, does ethnomethodology approach experience, cognition, and commonsense understanding? Let us begin with Garfinkel's (1988) suggestion:

> For ethnomethodology the objective reality of social facts, in that and just how it is every society's locally, endogenously produced, naturally organized, reflexively accountable, ongoing, practical achievement, being everywhere, always, only, exactly and entirely, members' work, with no time out, and with no possibility of evasion, hiding out, passing, postponement, or buy-outs, is *thereby* sociology's fundamental phenomenon. (p. 103)

For ethnomethodology, the "social facts" that the early Durkheim directed sociology toward are products of the ordinary social practices of members (natives) of society. These practices are orderly, organized phenomena that can be analyzed to reveal their methodical bases. Ethnomethodology thus investigates the methodical basis or orderly character of ordinary social activities. There is a concern to reveal the procedural basis of social activities; to examine *how* jurors reach decisions, *how* conversationalists take turns at talking, *how* astronomers make discoveries as part of a night's work in the observatory (Garfinkel, 1967; Sacks, Schegloff, & Jefferson, 1974; Garfinkel, Lynch, & Livingston, 1981).

The experiential emphasis found in ethnomethodology derives from its central interest in the recognition and production of social activities. How an activity is produced and internally organized is tied to the member's ability to recognize the activity as, for instance, a properly executed juror's decision. The recognition of an activity for whatever it may be is referred to by Garfinkel in the above quotation as its "reflexively accountable" feature. The details of the activity in some specific local context provide for its being seen as a "juror's decision," as a "reply" to a "question," or whatever. Making sense of social activities is something that is done locally, in situ, and is thus the practical accomplishment of members of society who cannot choose not to make sense. As Garfinkel notes, there is "no time out," "no possibility of evasion, hiding out, passing or postponement" (p. 103) for the member of society. In making sense; in seeing what someone or something means; in short, in engaging in commonsense understanding, the member of the society draws on social sources. Members of a society make sense of everyday events in much the same manner. There must therefore be some shared social means of making sense: These are the methods that ethnomethodology seeks to explicate. Thus, seeing a road sign as representing a "one-way street," or hearing an item of talk as a "question," or seeing "a lovely young lady alighting from a cab" as "a call girl arriving for a session" routinely involves the application by the member of certain sense-making methods (Sacks, 1972, p. 285). The investigation of these methods constitutes ethnomethodology's core topic of inquiry.

Making Sense of the Visual

An indication of how ethnomethodology can be applied to visual data is provided in Sharrock and Anderson's (1979) analysis of a collection of photographs of hospital directional signs. Written and pictorial signs are a common everyday feature of the public sphere of many cultures, and they serve a distinct practical purpose. Sharrock and Anderson treat the reading of a directional sign (e.g., "School of Radiography") as a practical activity done in the "here and now" of making one's way through hospital corridors. Thus, reading a sign is embedded in the practical concerns of anyone seeking to find a way to a chosen destination within the hospital. As Sharrock and Anderson suggest,

> When we think of people using signs it becomes obvious that the use they make of them is practical. They are not interested in the meaning of the sign but are interested in using the sign for some purpose. They are not interested in what signs in general mean, but in the use they can make of *This* sign, *Here* and *Now*. their reasoning is not theoretical and general but practical, particularised and in context. (p. 81)

Visual signs are usually encountered one at a time; at walking pace, people will not usually need to pause to read them before continuing on their way; they are read in situ and the reading is governed by a thoroughly practical motive ("How can I get to . . ."). As Sharrock and Anderson state, "We find a sense for the signs by finding a function for them to perform" (1979, p. 86), namely, to help us reach our destination. They draw attention to some of the generalized features of the sign reader's practical reasoning, including the features of location, juxtaposition, and sequence. Where signs occur and how they are sited next to each other or sequentially one after the other are plainly of relevance to finding one's destination. The signs have a "highly localised application: they point to places that are 'around here', even 'within this building'" (p. 86; see Figure 4.1).

Directional signs are often sequentially ordered as a tree structure. Signs encountered "earlier" en route are less discriminating than those encountered "later," as evidenced in the photograph of a sign to "Lecture Theatres" (Figure 4.1) that is followed later in sequence by signs to "Lecture Theatre 4" (Figure 4.2), "Lecture Theatre 5," and so forth. When collections of signs are close together, as in figures 4.1 and 4.2, color coding is frequently employed as a means of differentiating destinations. For instance, in Figure 4.1 the sign to hospital west block could be in orange, medical physics red, hospital south block gray, and lecture theatres blue, etc. All signs to lecture theatres are read in sequential order, but finding one's way to the lecture theatres may involve following blue-coded signs.

Sharrock and Anderson's (1979) study exemplifies certain key features of ethnomethodology's approach to visual experience. Reading a sign is a practical activity embedded in the business of "finding a way about" (p. 90). It involves particularized and localized courses of practical reasoning that

Figure 4.1. Hospital directional signs. Photo from Sharrock & Anderson.

are tied to this practical concern. Readers of signs do not make sense of them in a haphazard or idiosyncratic way, but rather engage in methodical practices of sense making that include orientations to the location, juxtaposition, and sequencing of the signs.

Reading a sign is one type of looking, but as Simmel (1921) reminded us, looking is a practice that is universal to social life. Ethnomethodologists have also analyzed the localized and in situ practices of ordinary glances (Sacks, 1989; Sudnow, 1972) and the visual assessments of moral character made by police working on the street (Sacks, 1972). In the last-named study, Sacks proposed that the police develop a knowledge of the "normal appearances" of the streets they work, i.e., "what everything proceeding as usual" ordinarily looks like. The officers' sense that something is "wrong" or "amiss" involves the employment of an "incongruity procedure" in which a perceived person or event (e.g., a truck parked outside a warehouse at midnight) contrasts with their expectation of normal appearances. Ethnomethodological studies are not necessarily restricted to the prosaic and mundane, however.

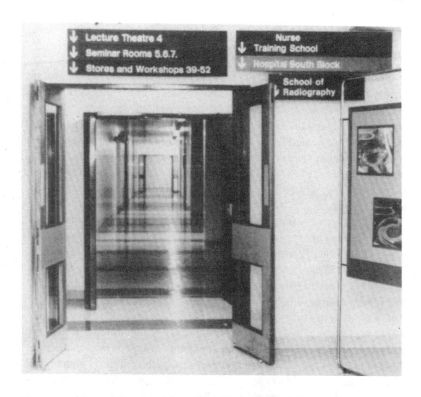

Figure 4.2. Hospital directional signs. Photo from Sharrock & Anderson.

We consider next some studies of scientific practice, including the process of scientific discovery, in which the visual dimension is prominent.

It was evident in our exposition of cognitive anthropology's consideration of color terminologies that color, a highly visual phenomenon, was rendered invisible: Color was explored as a terminological taxonomy making extensive use of visual metaphors. The following example of ethnomethodological research documents an almost reverse process. Astronomers' pulsars, which are invisible to the naked eye, are rendered seeable by the practices of computer graphics or digital image processing, making the invisible visible. The works we consider for this purpose (Garfinkel et al., 1981; Lynch, Livingston, & Garfinkel, 1983; Lynch & Edgerton, 1988) examine how natural scientists do the discovering work of science.

The Visual Representation of Scientific Theory and "Invisible" Data

Garfinkel and associates' (1981) study investigated the astronomical discovery of optical signals from Pulsar NP 0532 at Stewart Observatory in the United States in 1969. The scientists' conversations during the discovery were recorded, and then analyzed by Garfinkel and associates to find what the discussion revealed about the organization of doing discovery in science. The investigation showed how pulsars—natural objects—become cultural objects (Garfinkel et al., 1981) or, conversely, what is later referred to as the pulsar becoming attached to nature (Lynch et al., 1983). The descriptive and analytic language used by Garfinkel and his associates in both works is rich in the evocation of visual metaphors. For example, following Lévi-Strauss, they considered the expertise of *bricolage* as a metaphor for how science is done. The bricoleur constructs objects out of whatever materials are at hand. Following Merleau-Ponty (1968), the investigators considered the "intertwining" of worldly objects (the pulsar) and embodied practices (astronomical observations), which become a "potter's object." *Potter's object* is a metaphor used to explore how scientists make sense of an oscilloscopically displayed pulse and work with that developing image until they have processed a more definite thing, a pulsar, for all practical purposes. As Garfinkel et al. (1981) suggest, "This strong orderliness of the pulsar 'is in the practitioners hands,' and this orderliness offers itself in elaborating details of attempts, repairs, and discards of locally motivated and locally occasioned modifications on the pulsar's existing material 'shape'" (p. 137).

One aspect of Garfinkel's research was to explore the essentially practical work of visualizing the data, a process described as "seeing the physics" (Lynch & Edgerton, 1988, p. 213). The astronomer's task of exhibiting, analyzing, and accounting for the data as an optical pulsar, making sense of the materials, is the discovery: "The gorgeousness of their discovery is that they get access to the intertwining. Their achievement is the apt efficacy of finding and demonstrating—It—again in astronomically established details" (Garfinkel et al., 1981, p. 142).

Another strand of investigation by Lynch and Edgerton (1988) considered the more directly empirical issue of the extent to which digital image processing, "seeing the physics," constitutes an integral and aesthetic dimension of contemporary astronomy. This research examines the developing craft within science of constructing pictorial and graphic representations and models for showing ideas. Digital image processing now occupies a central place in astronomical research, with astronomers both engaged in composing the visuals, "showing the physics," and analyzing graphic and pictorial representations of the phenomenon investigated. Lynch and Edgerton indicate how astronomers use digital image processing to prepare visual representations of the investigated phenomenon for various analytic purposes.

Computer graphics frequently employ color displays, which involve the innovative use of false colors, enhanced true color, and other techniques of visual representation. As Lynch and Edgerton (1988) argue, "colour combinations can be used to 'bring out' thematic features in a field, or to suppress backgrounds" (p. 189). In a section titled "pictures as narrative accounts," they argue that astronomers use visual representations to do certain types of analytical work, and that they tie in these visuals with their data, shaping the presentation of visual images in a manner appropriate to the argument being pursued:

> Captions do not simply tell what is "in" a picture: they orient viewers to similarities, contrasts, and other relevancies; they supply substantive identities for distinguishable features; and they supply metaphors, extrinsic connections, and genealogies which instruct viewers' understanding of what they are being shown. As suggested by the cliche, "a picture is worth a thousand words," it is common place to view captions as working off of information supplied in pictures, but digital image processing demonstrates that the opposite can just as readily obtain. The features of a picture can be adjusted to fit a caption. (p. 202)

For us, this constitutes a reformulation of the previously noted problem of realism. To what extent are these products of computer graphics operating as a mirror of nature, or are they actually constituting natural scientific knowledge of nature? Lynch and Edgerton remind us, "If, indeed, astronomers make use of colour and other elements of composition ·as abstractable representational media, rather than as mirrored properties of objects, they do so as committed realists, aiming to endow their compositions with naturalistic adequacy" (1988, p. 214). From our review of research into visual representations within astronomy—seeing the physics—it seems that such representations are methods for adding visual dimensions to an investigated phenomenon, in order to make the phenomenon more readily accessible. Data are transformed into a visual form that then constitutes our experience of the phenomenon.

An Epistemological Epilogue

We conclude this chapter with some tentative observations concerning the status of ethnomethodology within current debates rising from anthropological postmodernism. Postmodernism is a multidisciplinary, markedly eclectic enterprise, which has diverse philosophical roots ranging from "critical" Marxism to metaphorically rich Nietzschean orientations and Heideggerian phenomenology. Its philosophical energy emanates from debates between Lyotard, Habermas, and Jameson (Lyotard, 1984; Habermas, 1984; Jameson, 1983). Our concern, however, is only with anthropological postmodernism, and for our purposes it is convenient to summarize its concerns as broadly methodological and focused on the character of ethnography and the construction of ethnographic reports. This methodological concern arises from postmodernism's disenchantment with positivistic science and its language (a general antipositivism that ethnomethodology also shares).

Two other strands of anthropological postmodernism are of significance for ethnographic methodology. Both postmodernism and ethnomethodology argue that theoretical, methodological, and substantive issues are inseparable: Both are concerned, although with slightly differing emphases, with the issue of reflexivity. Garfinkel's notion of the reflexivity of accounts emphasizes how ethnographic findings cannot be understood apart from members' methods for making sense and producing social activities (Wieder, 1974). Anthropological postmodernism stresses the central role of the ethnographic text in mediating what passes as ethnographic knowledge. As Van Maanen (1988) pointed out, although fieldwork consists of collecting ethnographic materials, writing ethnography is desk work, and thus the consideration of the conventions and rhetorics of ethnographic texts becomes a pressing concern (p. 4). Second, given the presumed demise of the relevance of science for ethnography, anthropological postmodernism seeks to explore the boundaries of the ethnographically possible. It considers what ethnography might encompass and what form of discourse it might become. One of the more radical proposals is that ethnography might become a form of poetics (Tyler, 1986).

It would have been satisfying to end with a demonstration of what anthropological postmodernism might contribute to a study of visual experience, but thus far the tradition has offered few indications of making such contributions. Dwyer's *Moroccan Dialogues* (1982) is frequently cited as exhibiting a seminal character, but it also demonstrates, returning to points made by Mead and Tyler, that in "disciplines of words," "language does the work of the eyes." Indeed, it seems that the bulk of anthropological post-modernism's concerns are with textual strategies and written styles of discourse used in ethnographic description (note the title of one influential text: *Writing Culture,* Clifford & Marcus, 1986; Spencer, 1989).

We argued in chapter 1 that anthropology and sociology make little use of assorted visual materials. Although the statement is accurate in a literal and material sense, postmodernism suggests that metaphorically the visual exercises a very powerful sway on how experience is expressed and how theory, method, and data are represented. The language of science is replete with a rich visual imagery and root metaphors for expressing knowledge (Yates, 1966; Fabian, 1983). For example, Goffman's works (1963a, 1963b, 1971) draw our attention to focused and unfocused interaction, stigma, and tie signs; and yet only in *Gender Advertisements* (1979) does he *show* the visual. More classically, Herbert Spencer used the visual metaphor of a tree to analyze social evolution (Peele, 1971). Here, in Lévi-Strauss's sense, an item from nature was drawn upon to think and express certain features of society and culture. Visual metaphors such as trees are indeed good to think with and integral to the analytical roots of scientific thought, as evident in the use of branching diagrams and the like to express relations between parts of a system. Indeed, the notion of cognitive map is itself a visualist metaphor. As the philosopher John Locke (1689/1964) maintained, "The perception of the mind . . . is most aptly explained by words relating to the sight" (p. 227). Disciplines of words are thus founded on a visualist epistemology.

The debates about postmodernism are in their infancy, still rather speculative, and have yet to suggest clear directions for the future of ethnography. One possible outcome is a pastiche of research strategies. At the start, ethnomethodology was similarly programmatic and polemical, but since then it has produced an impressive catalog of research. In one sense, anthropological postmodernism now occupies a similar position to early ethnomethodology on a whole range of criteria, and for us it is puzzling that given their common epistemological concerns, postmodernism has failed to notice the lessons that might be learned from ethnomethodology.

Ethnomethodology, in common with anthropological postmodernism, is strikingly antipositivistic, but from a consistent philosophical base, even if occasionally some of its work does evidence a minimal positivistic slippage. From certain of the programmatic statements of anthropological postmodernism, such as Tyler and others' suggestions of poetics, it is difficult to envisage precisely what its ethnography might become. Ethnomethodology has spawned two major research programs centering on studies of work (e.g.,

Garfinkel, 1986) and the analysis of conversation (e.g., Atkinson & Heritage, 1984). Moreover, ethnomethodology has something to offer postmodernism with its analyses of how fieldwork is actually accomplished (Wieder, 1974; Stoddart, 1986) and how sociological works are constructed as persuasive texts (Anderson & Sharrock, 1982, 1984).

It seems to us that in an epistemological sense, anthropological postmodernism has discovered the wheel in surprising and blissful ignorance of its earlier construction. To us this is shockingly wasteful of analytical endeavor, particularly given that the line between ethnographic work in anthropology and sociology is blurring. In conclusion, we suggest that students of anthropological postmodernism may find products of ethnomethodology, ranging from conversation analysis to Blum and McHugh's "theorizing" (Blum, 1974, Blum & McHugh, 1983), instructive and philosophically sophisticated for tackling certain of the epistemological problems they have uncovered, as if for the first time.

REFERENCES

Agee, J., & Evans, W. 1941. *Let us now praise famous men.* Boston: Houghton Mifflin.

Anderson, N. 1923. *The hobo.* Chicago: University of Chicago Press.

Anderson, R. J., Hughes, J. A., & Sharrock, W. W. 1985. *The sociology game: An introduction to sociological reasoning.* London: Longman.

Anderson, R. J., & Sharrock, W. W. 1982. Sociological work: Some procedures sociologists use for organising phenomena. *Social Analysis, 11,* 79-93.

Anderson, R. J. & Sharrock, W. W. 1984. Analytic work: Aspects of the organisation of conversational data. *Journal for the Theory of Social Behaviour, 14*(1), 103-124.

Atkinson, J. M., & Heritage, J. (Eds.). 1984. *Structures of social action: Studies in conversation analysis.* Cambridge, UK: Cambridge University Press.

Barley, N. 1986. *The innocent anthropologist: Notes from a mud hut.* Harmondsworth, UK: Penguin.

Barley, S. R. 1983a. The codes of the dead: The semiotics of funeral work. *Urban Life, 12*(1), 3-31.

Barley, S. R. 1983b. Semiotics and the study of occupational and organizational cultures. *Administrative Science Quarterly, 28,* 393-413.

Bateson, G. 1936. *Naven.* Cambridge, UK: Cambridge University Press.

Bateson, G., & Mead, M. 1942. *Balinese character: A photographic analysis* (Special Publications, vol. 2). New York: New York Academy of Sciences.

Becker, H. S. 1975. Photography and sociology. *Afterimage, 3*(May-June), 22-32. (Reprinted in Becker, 1986)

Becker, H. S. 1978. Do photographs tell the truth? *Afterimage, 5*(February), 9-13. (Reprinted in Becker, 1986)

Becker, H. S. 1979. Preface. In J. Wagner (Ed.), *Images of information: Still photography in the social sciences* (pp. 7-8). Beverly Hills, CA: Sage.

Becker, H. S. (Ed.). 1981. *Exploring society photographically.* Chicago: University of Chicago Press.

Becker, H. S. 1986. *Doing things together: Selected papers.* Evanston, IL: Northwestern University Press.

Berelson, B. 1952. *Content analysis in communication research.* New York: Free Press.

Berger, J. 1989. Appearances. In J. Berger & J. Mohr, *Another way of telling* (pp. 81-129). Cambridge, UK: Granta.

Berlin, B., & Kay, P. 1969. *Basic color terms.* Berkeley and Los Angeles: University of California Press.

Bittner, E. 1973. Objectivity and realism in sociology. In G. Psathas (Ed.), *Phenomenological sociology: Issues and applications* (pp. 109-125). New York: John Wiley.

Blum, A. 1974. *Theorizing.* London: Heinemann.

Blum, A., & McHugh, P. 1983. *Self-reflection in the arts and sciences.* Atlantic Highlands, NJ: Humanities Press.

Boas, F. 1927. *Primitive art.* Cambridge, MA: Harvard University Press.

Boas, F., & Hunt, G. 1905. *Kwakiutl texts* (*Memoirs,* vol. 5). New York: American Museum of Natural History.

72

Boas, F. & Hunt, G. 1908. *Kwakiutl texts* (2nd series, *Memoirs*, vol. 14). New York: American Museum of Natural History.

Burgelin, O. 1972. Structuralist analysis and mass communication. In D. McQuail (Ed.), *The sociology of mass communications* (pp. 313-328). Harmondsworth, UK: Penguin.

Chagnon, N. 1974. *Studying the Yanomamo.* New York: Holt, Rinehart & Winston.

Cicourel, A. V. 1964. *Method and measurement in sociology.* New York: Free Press.

Clifford, J., & Marcus, G. E. (Eds.). 1986. *Writing culture: The poetics and politics of ethnography.* Berkeley: University of California Press.

Collier, J., Jr., & Collier, M. 1986. *Visual anthropology: Photography as a research method.* Albuquerque: University of New Mexico Press.

Conklin, H. C. 1955. Hanunoo color categories. *Southwestern Journal of Anthropology, 11*(4), 339-344.

Cordwell, J. M. (Ed.). 1979. *The visual arts: Plastic and graphic.* The Hague: Mouton.

Coser, L. A., Nock, S. L., Steffan, P. A., & Rhea, B. 1987. *Introduction to sociology* (2nd ed.). San Diego, CA: Harcourt Brace Jovanovich.

Coulter, J. 1973. Language and the conceptualization of meaning. *Sociology, 7*(2), 173-189.

Coulter, J. 1979. *The social construction of mind: Studies in ethnomethodology and linguistic philosophy.* London: Macmillan.

Coulter, J. 1989. *Mind in action.* Cambridge, UK: Polity.

Curtis, E. S. 1915. *The North American Indian, 10 (Kwakiutl).* New York: Johnson.

Duerr, H. P. 1985. *Dreamtime.* Oxford, UK: Blackwell.

Dwyer, K. 1982. *Moroccan dialogues.* Baltimore, MD: Johns Hopkins University Press.

Eglin, P. 1980. *Talk and taxonomy: A methodological comparison of ethnosemantics and ethnomethodology with reference to terms for Canadian doctors.* Amsterdam: John Benjamins.

Evans-Pritchard, E. E. 1937. *Witchcraft, oracles and magic among the Azande.* Oxford, UK: Oxford University Press.

Evans-Pritchard, E. E. 1940. *The Nuer.* Oxford, UK: Clarendon.

Fabian, J. 1983. *Time and the other: How anthropology makes its object.* New York: Columbia University Press.

Firth, R. 1936. *We the Tikopia.* London: Allen and Unwin.

Firth, R. 1973. *Symbols: Public and private.* London: Allen and Unwin.

Frake, C. O. 1969. The ethnographic study of cognitive systems. In S. A. Tyler (Ed.), *Cognitive anthropology.* New York: Holt, Rinehart & Winston.

Garfinkel, H. 1967. *Studies in ethnomethodology.* Englewood Cliffs, NJ: Prentice-Hall.

Garfinkel, H. 1968. On the origins of the term "ethnomethodology." In R. Turner (Ed.), *Ethnomethodology: Selected readings* (pp. 15-18). Harmondsworth, UK: Penguin.

Garfinkel, H. (Ed.). 1986. *Ethnomethodological studies of work* (pp. 28-41). London: Routledge and Kegan Paul.

Garfinkel, H. 1988. Evidence for locally produced, naturally accountable phenomena of order*, logic, reason, meaning, method, etc. in and as of the essential quiddity of immortal ordinary society (I of IV): An announcement of studies. *Sociological Theory, 6*(1), 103-109.

Garfinkel, H., Lynch, M., & Livingston, E. 1981. The work of a discovering science construed with materials from the optically discovered pulsar. *Philosophy of the Social Sciences, 11,* 131-158.

Geertz, C. 1973. *The interpretation of cultures: Selected essays.* New York: Basic Books.

Geertz, C. 1976. From the native's point of view. In P. Rabinow & W. M. Sullivan (Eds.), *Interpretive social science: A reader* (pp. 225-241). Berkeley: University of California Press, 1979.

Gerbner, G., Holsti, O. R., Krippendorff, K., Paisley, W. J., & Stone, P. J. 1969. *The analysis of communication content: Developments in scientific theories and computer techniques.* New York: John Wiley.

Glassner, B., & Corzine, J. 1982. Library research as fieldwork: A strategy for qualitative content analysis. *Sociology and Social Research, 66,* 305-319.

Gluckman, M. 1965. *The ideas in Barotse jurisprudence.* New Haven, CT: Yale University Press.

Goffman, E. 1961. *Asylums: Essays on the social situation of mental patients and other inmates.* Garden City, NY: Anchor.

Goffman, E. 1963a. *Behavior in public places: Notes on the social organization of gatherings.* New York: Free Press.

Goffman, E. 1963b. *Stigma: Notes on the management of spoiled identity.* Englewood Cliffs, NJ: Prentice-Hall.

Goffman, E. 1971. *Relations in public: Microstudies of the public order.* New York: Basic Books.

Goffman, E. 1974. *Frame analysis: An essay on the organization of experience.* Cambridge, MA: Harvard University Press.

Goffman, E. 1979. *Gender advertisements.* London: Macmillan.

Gombrich, E. H. 1960. *Art and illusion: A study in the psychology of pictorial representation.* Oxford, UK: Phaidon.

Goodenough, W. 1957. Cultural anthropology and linguistics. In D. Hymes (Ed.), *Language in culture and society* (pp. 36-39). New York: Harper & Row, 1964.

Gregor, T. 1977. *Mehinaku: The drama of daily life in a Brazilian Indian village.* Chicago: University of Chicago Press.

Habermas, J. 1984. *The theory of communicative action, Vol. 1: Reason and the rationalization of society.* Cambridge, UK: Polity.

Haddon, A. C. 1895. *Evolution in art.* London: Watts.

Holsti, O. R. 1969. *Content analysis for the social sciences and humanities.* Reading, MA: Addison-Wesley.

Husserl, E. 1960. *Cartesian meditations.* The Hague: Martinus Nijhoff.

Husserl, E. 1970. *Logical investigations.* New York: Humanities Press.

Husserl, E. 1973. *Experience and judgement.* Evanston, IL: Northwestern University Press.

Jameson, F. 1983. Postmodernism and consumer society. In H. Foster (Ed.), *The anti-aesthetic: Essays on postmodern culture* (pp. 111-125). Port Townsend, WA: Bay Press.

Konig, R. 1973. *A la mode: On the social psychology of fashion.* New York: Seabury.

Kracauer, S. 1952. The challenge of qualitative content analysis. *Public Opinion Quarterly, 16*(4), 631-642.

Krippendorff, K. 1980. *Content analysis: An introduction to its methodology.* Beverly Hills, CA: Sage.

Lévi-Strauss, C. 1969. *The elementary structures of kinship.* Boston: Beacon.

Lévi-Strauss, C. 1978. *Structural anthropology* (Vol. 2). Harmondsworth, UK: Peregrine.

Lévi-Strauss, C. 1983. *The way of the masks.* London: Cape.

Locke, J. 1964. *An essay concerning human understanding.* New York: Meridian. (Originally published 1689)

Lynch, M., & Edgerton, S. Y. 1988. Aesthetics and digital image processing: Representational craft in contemporary astronomy. In G. Fyfe & J. Law (Eds.), *Picturing power: Visual depiction and social relations* (Sociological Review Monograph No. 35, pp. 184-220). London: Routledge and Kegan Paul.

Lynch, M., Livingston, E., & Garfinkel, H. 1983. Temporal order in laboratory work. In K. Knorr-Cetina & M. Mulkay (Eds.), *Science observed* (pp. 205-238). Beverly Hills: Sage.

Lyotard, J-F. 1984. *The postmodern condition: A report on knowledge.* Manchester, UK: Manchester University Press.

Malinowski, B. 1929. *The sexual life of savages.* London: Routledge and Kegan Paul.

Mann, P. H. 1985. *Methods of social investigation.* Oxford: Blackwell.

Manning, P. K. 1987. *Semiotics and fieldwork.* Newbury Park, CA: Sage.

Marcus, G. E., & Fischer, M.M.J. 1986. *Anthropology as cultural critique.* Chicago: University of Chicago Press.

Mauss, M. 1966. *The gift.* London: Routledge and Kegan Paul.

Mead, M. 1975. Visual anthropology in a discipline of words. In P. Hockings (Ed.), *Principles of visual anthropology* (pp. 4-10). The Hague: Mouton.

Merleau-Ponty, M. 1968. *The visible and the invisible.* Evanston, IL: Northwestern University Press.

Modelski, S. 1983. Translator's note. In C. Lévi-Strauss, *The way of the masks* (p. v). London: Cape.

Morley, D. 1980. *The "nationwide" audience: Structure and decoding.* London: British Film Institute.

Morley, D. 1981. The "Nationwide" Audience—A critical postscript. *Screen Education, 39,* 3-14.

Ohrn, K. B. 1980. *Dorothea Lange and the documentary tradition.* Baton Rouge: Louisiana State University Press.

Peele, J.D.Y. 1971. *Herbert Spencer: The evolution of a sociologist.* London: Heinemann.

Pike, K. L. 1954. *Language in relation to a unified theory of the structure of human behavior.* Glendale, CA: Summer Institute of Linguistics.

Platt, J. 1981. Reading data: Evidence and proof in documentary research (Parts 1 & 2). *Sociological Review, 29*(1), 29-66.

Radcliffe-Brown, A. R. 1922. *The Andaman Islanders: A study in social anthropology.* Cambridge, UK: Cambridge University Press.

Richardson, J., & Kroeber, A. L. 1940. Three centuries of women's dress fashions: A quantitative analysis. *Anthropological Records, 5*(2), 111-153.

Riis, J. A. 1890. *How the other half lives: Studies among the tenements of New York.* New York: Scribner's.

Rivers, W.H.R. 1901. Introduction and vision. In A. C. Haddon (Ed.), *Reports on the Cambridge Anthropological Expedition to the Torres Straits* (Vol. 2, pp. 1-146). Cambridge: Cambridge University Press.

Robinson, D. E. 1976. Fashions in the shaving and trimming of the beard: The men of the *Illustrated London News, 1842-1972. American Journal of Sociology, 81*(5), 1133-1141.

Rorty, R. 1979. *Philosophy and the mirror of nature.* Princeton, NJ: Princeton University Press.

Ruby, J. 1976. In a pic's eye: Interpretive strategies for deriving significance and meaning from photographs. *Afterimage, 3*(March), 5-7.

Sacks, H. 1972. Notes on the police assessment of moral character. In D. Sudnow (Ed.) *Studies in social interaction* (pp. 280-293). New York: Free Press.

Sacks, H. 1989. Lecture eleven: On exchanging glances. *Human Studies, 12*(3-4), 333-348.

Sacks, H, Schegloff, E., & Jefferson, G. 1974. A simplest systematics for the organization of turn-taking in conversation. *Language, 50*(4), 696-735.

Sapir, E. 1931. Fashion. In E.R.A. Seligman (Ed.), *Encyclopedia of the Social Sciences* (Vol. 6, pp. 139-144). New York: Macmillan.

Saussure, F. de. 1959. *Course in general linguistics.* New York: Philosophical Library.

Schutz, A. 1967. *The phenomenology of the social world.* Evanston, IL: Northwestern University Press.

Scott, J. 1990. *A matter of record: Documentary sources in social research.* Cambridge, UK: Polity.

Sekula, A. 1975. On the invention of photographic meaning. *Artforum, 13*(January), 36-45.

Sharrock, W. W., & Anderson, D. 1979. Directional hospital signs as sociological data. *Information Design Journal, 1*(2), 81-94.

Signorile, V. 1987. Capitulating to captions: The verbal transformation of visual images. *Human Studies, 10,* 281-310.

Simmel, G. 1921. Sociology of the senses: Visual interaction. In R. E. Park & E. W. Burgess (Eds.), *Introduction to the science of sociology* (pp. 356-361). Chicago: University of Chicago Press. (Originally published in German in 1908)

Simmel, G. 1957. Fashion. *American Journal of Sociology, 62,* 541-558. (Reprint of translation from *International Quarterly, 10* [New York, 1904])

Sontag, S. 1979. *On photography.* Harmondsworth, UK: Penguin.

Spencer, J. 1989. Anthropology as a kind of writing. *Man, 24*(1), 145-164.

Spradley, J. P. 1980. *Participant observation.* New York: Holt, Rinehart & Winston.

Spradley, J. P., & Mann, B. J. 1975. *The cocktail waitress: Women's work in a man's world.* New York: John Wiley.

Stasz, C. 1979. The early history of visual sociology. In J. Wagner (Ed.). *Images of information: Still photography in the social sciences* (pp. 119-136). Beverly Hills, CA: Sage.

Stoddart, K. 1986. The presentation of everyday life: Some textual strategies for "adequate ethnography." *Urban Life, 15,* 103-121.

Strathern, A., & Strathern, M. 1971. *Self-decoration in Mount Hagen.* London: Duckworth.

Sudnow, D. 1972. Temporal parameters of interpersonal observation. In D. Sudnow (Ed.), *Studies in social interaction* (pp. 259-279). New York: Free Press.

Sumner, C. 1979. *Reading ideologies: An investigation into the Marxist theory of law and ideology.* London: Academic Press.

Tagg, J. 1988. *The burden of representation: Essays on photographies and histories.* London: Macmillan.

Thrasher, F. 1927. *The gang.* Chicago: University of Chicago Press.

Turner, V. 1967. *The forest of symbols.* Ithaca, NY: Cornell University Press.

Tyler, S. A. (Ed.). 1969. *Cognitive anthropology.* New York: Holt, Rinehart & Winston.

Tyler, S. A. 1986. Post-modern ethnography: From document of the occult to occult document. In J. Clifford & G. F. Marcus (Eds.), *Writing culture: The poetics and politics of ethnography* (pp. 122-140). Berkeley: University of California Press.

Van Maanen, J. C. 1988. *Tales of the field: On writing ethnography.* Chicago: University of Chicago Press.

Waksler, F. 1986. Studying children: Phenomenological insights. *Human Studies, 9,* 71-82.

Walens, S. 1981. *Feasting with cannibals.* Princeton, NJ: Princeton University Press.

Wheeler, S. (Ed.). 1969. *On record: Files and dossiers in American society.* New York: Russell Sage Foundation.

Whyte, W. F. 1943. *Street corner society.* Chicago: University of Chicago Press.

Wieder, D. L. 1971. On meaning by rule. In J. D. Douglas (Ed.), *Understanding everyday life: Toward the reconstruction of sociological knowledge* (pp. 107-135). London: Routledge and Kegan Paul.

Wieder, D. L. 1974. *Language and social reality: The case of telling the convict code.* The Hague: Mouton.

Williams, R. 1976. *Communications.* Harmondsworth, UK: Penguin.

Williamson, J. 1978. *Decoding advertisements: Ideology and meaning in advertising.* London: Marion Boyars.

Wittgenstein, L. 1953. *Philosophical investigations.* Oxford, UK: Blackwell.

Yates, F. A. 1966. *The art of memory.* Chicago: University of Chicago Press.

Zimmerman, D. H., & Pollner, M. 1971. The everyday world as a phenomenon. In J. D. Douglas (Ed.), *Understanding everyday life: Toward the reconstruction of sociological knowledge* (pp. 80-103). London: Routledge and Kegan Paul.

ABOUT THE AUTHORS

MICHAEL S. BALL is Senior Lecturer in Anthropology and Sociology at Staffordshire Polytechnic. He studied for a B.A. (Hons) at Manchester Polytechnic and then researched first at the University of Salford for his M.Sc. and then at the University of Manchester for his Ph.D. He has taught undergraduates and postgraduates at Staffordshire Polytechnic, and at Salford and Manchester universities. In 1986-1987, he was an Honorary Visiting Research Fellow in the Department of Social Anthropology at the University of Manchester. His research interests and publications are in the area of qualitative analysis, encompassing ethnomethodology and anthropological postmodernism and a general concern with ethnographic investigation extending from studies of work in Britain to Tibetan Buddhism.

GREGORY W. H. SMITH, B.Sc., Ph.D., was educated at the University of Salford where he is now a Lecturer in Sociology. His research interests and publications concern theoretical and empirical aspects of the interpretive and ethnographic sociologies. He is currently working on a book on Goffman's sociology.

The authors have worked together on several projects, ranging from studies of queues to the present book.